PRAISE FOR
LEADING THROUGH THE WATER

"The ritual of baptism has often been reduced to a symbolic 'rite of passage' into a local congregation. Paul Galbreath, reaching into memory and history, has called us as readers into the recovery of the sacred and the transformational as inherent ingredients in this formative event. We all recover in these pages a sense of our full conversion as followers of The Way."
    —*Daniel G. Bagby, Theodore F. Adams Emeritus Professor of Pastoral care, Baptist Theological Seminary at Richmond*

"In this deep and refreshing work, Galbreath taps the well-spring of ancient Christian tradition, distills clear analysis of our contemporary setting, and draws on a great reservoir of personal and pastoral experience—all to show that Christian life is baptismal life. The church and world are thirsty for such wisdom."
    —*David Gambrell, Associate for Worship, Office of Theology and Worship, Presbyterian Church (USA)*

"With vivid stories and provocative questions, Paul Galbreath leads us on a journey through the waters of baptism. Focusing on how this ancient practice shapes Christian disciples for today, Galbreath illumines baptism as the pattern of a whole life, rooted in God's mercy and turned in compassion toward the world. These reflections will shake and revive you like fresh rain."
    —*Martha Moore-Keish, Associate Professor of Theology, Columbia Theological Seminary*

"Paul Galbreath invites us on a joy-filled, expansive journey that connects the sacrament of baptism with the ongoing life of discipleship. Paul's accessible style links biblical narrative and ancient voices with contemporary experience and the world, in which we are to live out our baptismal identity. As these voices come together, we find a challenging invitation to transform congregational worship and response. Ever the good teacher, Paul encourages us to live out our baptismal identity both within and beyond the walls of our churches."
—*Walt Lichtenberger, Lead Pastor,*
St. James Lutheran, Burnsville, MN

"With a rich interplay of biblical story, history, and clear articulation of our common baptismal vocation, *Leading through the Water* will captivate, challenge and inspire leaders and congregants alike to greater awareness of the power of the Spirit at work in community—for the sake of the world's forgotten. Live into Christ's call alive in each chapter."
—*Lynn Longfield, General Presbyter,*
Presbytery of Olympia

Other Books in the Vital Worship, Healthy Congregations Series

Leading through the Water

Leading through the Water

Paul Galbreath

FOREWORD BY CRAIG A. SATTERLEE

Herndon, Virginia
www.alban.org

The Alban Institute
2121 Cooperative Way, Suite 100
Herndon, VA 20171

Unless otherwise noted, all Scripture quotations are from the New Revised Standard Version of the Bible, copyright © 1989, Division of Christian Education of the National Council of the Churches of Christ in the United States of America, and are used by permission.

Cover Design by Tobias Becker, Bird Box Design.

Library of Congress Cataloging-in-Publication Data

Galbreath, Paul.
  Leading through the water / Paul Galbreath.
    p. cm.
  Includes bibliographical references.
  ISBN 978-1-56699-413-2
  1. Baptism. I. Title.
  BV811.3.G35 2011
  265'.1--dc22

                                    2011004931

11   12   13   14   15   VP   5   4   3   2   1

In memory of and thanksgiving for the life of Anna Ayers,
friend and companion on the way.

Contents

Foreword

A LONG TIME AGO, when I was an assistant pastor, I was charged with coming up with a theme for our congregation's midweek Lenten worship services. The previous Easter, we had our first Vigil and, during the affirmation of baptism, I got everyone really wet. Some members of the congregation, including the head of the altar guild, who cleaned up my mess, thought it would be good to keep Lent with a sermon series on baptism. When I proposed baptism as a Lenten theme to the senior pastor, he expressed concern that baptism was not a big enough subject to fill six Wednesdays in Lent. I wish I could have handed him Paul Galbreath's book.

My senior pastor's concern that baptism was not big enough was not unfounded. For a long time the church worked very hard to make baptism smaller. In many places baptism was removed from the Sunday worship service and became a private family matter. I have seen baptism consist of nothing more than three drops of water administered with a rose in the name of the triune God. The baby never got wet, and Mom got the flower. Baptismal fonts were tucked away in closets when not in use, in the same way that baptismal certificates are tucked away in Bibles until they are needed—as proof that one can be married in the church and as an assurance that a deceased loved one is bound for heaven. Then, about thirty years ago, the church rediscovered baptism. Pastors tell the faithful to remember their baptism, to live out their baptism. The church works hard to make baptism bigger. In response, many Christians honestly ask, "How can I live out what I do not remember?"

In *Leading through the Water*, Paul Galbreath joyously leads faith communities in a conversation aimed at helping enliven their faith and sense of mission by making baptism bigger. For starters, Paul wants us to give up any idea that baptism is an isolated event that, for many of us, happened long ago. "From the baptismal water," Paul writes, "we move in hope toward God's reign by practicing hospitality, caring for creation, and providing food, shelter, and healing to those in need. This baptismal life, this water journey that we share, is an adventure as we move together into God's future." Like an experienced guide, Paul leads us on this journey, not taking the trip for us or telling us what we should see and do, but pointing out landmarks and equipping us to make the baptismal journey with the members of our faith community. Paul wants us to arrive at an appreciation of baptism not as a single occasion but as a distinctive way of life within a faith community.

Paul's goal is to explore with us what he calls "sacramental ethics" by connecting baptismal practices with daily life so that congregations provide an alternative, gospel witness to the world. He is convinced that when we are baptized, God gives us a new identity that reflects Christ and therefore is frequently at odds with our culture. For example, in a world torn by division, where we are taught to distrust those who differ from us, the unity in Christ that God gives in baptism compels Christians and congregations to step out of our comfort zones and connect with brothers and sisters in Christ in unfamiliar settings, cultures, and circumstances. The hospitality with which Christ welcomes us at the font leads us gratefully to extend Christ's hospitality to others in concrete ways. Anointed with the Holy Spirit, we are given talents and abilities to use in service to others rather than to benefit ourselves. In a culture that focuses on the individual, baptism leads to a shared life in community. In a culture focused on celebrity, baptism calls us to stand with the poor through concrete acts of hospitality and generosity. In a culture of virtual relationships, where our tendency is to complain and our *modus operandi* is to distrust, baptism insists that we break bread together, praise God, and extend goodwill. Our holy use of water in worship to give new life reminds us that all water—all creation—is God's holy, gracious, life-giving gift, which needs to be protected rather than exploited. Embracing

Christ means relinquishing certain attitudes and activities, including cultural notions of success.

Because baptism is a lifelong journey, this book is organized as the journey that those coming to faith in Christ take. In one way or another, all adults first inquire about who Christians are and what they do. In time, they prepare for baptism, are baptized, and spend time reflecting on the meaning of this rite. The foundation of this journey is not theology but practice. Paul reflects on the ways Christians and congregations have shared and continue to share the faith, prepare people to be baptized, administer or celebrate baptism, and make disciples. The book's journey is punctuated with vivid stories and concrete examples from Scripture, church history, and real-life congregations. Experience and information join in proclamation as Paul concludes each chapter with a sermon. More than learning from this book, you will receive the good news of the gospel, hope, sustenance, and renewal.

"Are you ready to change your life?" In some times and places, the wording of this question might be more churchly, but that's the bottom-line question the church asks candidates for baptism. Paul Galbreath asks this question of us. If our answer is yes, Paul invites us to undertake a journey of discipleship saturated with baptismal images by gathering a cadre of traveling companions—those long in the faith and those unsure that they are ready to set out. Bring along a Bible to serve as your compass. Reading these pages, you will refer to it often. And get ready to be changed. For Paul would tell us that we stand with the needy and suffering, break bread and extend hospitality to those different from ourselves, and use our gifts for others not to help or change them. We do these things so that others might help us reexamine our individual and congregational lives in light of the gospel. In the process, we will "grow in the grace and knowledge of our Lord and Savior Jesus Christ" (2 Pet. 3:18). This is the gift and power of Christ's saving work in baptism. Baptism is simply that big!

CRAIG A. SATTERLEE
Dean, ACTS Doctor of Ministry in Preaching Program

Preface

FOR THE PAST FEW YEARS, my teaching and writing have centered on what I call sacramental ethics, or how worship connects with daily life. I am particularly interested in discovering links between the sacraments of baptism and communion and the world around us. This passion for showing how faith helps us see the world around us in a new way grows out of a concern that far too often we adopt one way of speaking and acting inside a church sanctuary on Sunday morning and another way when we return to what we often call the "real world." When we separate church life from daily life, we marginalize the gospel and its message of incarnation, the good news that God is with us at all times and places in our lives.

For Christians, the radical portrait of God's presence in our lives centers on the Christ story, starting with the long-ago birth of Jesus to young, poor parents. The focus of this story is Jesus's public ministry to the poor, sick, demonic, and estranged. This image of incarnational ministry grows out of the biblical witness portraying Jesus's confrontation with the political and religious forces of his times. While it leads Jesus to conflict and crucifixion, the Gospels wrap this narrative in the cloth of resurrection hope.

Today, as in earlier times, communities of faith struggle to live out this vision of incarnational life in ways that point to God's presence among us. This book demonstrates one way of linking baptismal practice to daily life as congregations provide an alternative witness to the cultural voices around us. At the same time, it expands the vision of baptism from a single occasion to a distinctive way of life within a community of faith.

I am particularly grateful to communities that have taught me and helped me learn more about this vision of life shared together. Ten years as a pastor in the Pacific Northwest helped me gain a clearer perspective about the church's changing role in society and the need for the church to develop a stronger voice about our Christian identity. My thanks to congregations in Clatskanie, Woodburn, and Warrenton, Oregon, and Tacoma, Washington, for sharing this journey with me. During the years that I worked in the Office of Theology and Worship of the Presbyterian Church (USA), I settled on the language of sacramental ethics. My thanks go to colleagues there who helped me sharpen the language and focus of those initial forays (especially Chip Andrus, Martha Moore-Keish, and Steve Shussett). For the past several years, I have taught worship at Union Presbyterian Seminary in Richmond, Virginia. In particular, I am indebted to students in my master of divinity classes on baptism and to doctor of ministry students in seminars on the sacraments who worked with me on portions of this material. Two colleagues have been particularly supportive throughout this project: Beverly Zink-Sawyer, my regular teaching partner at Union, and Cláudio Carvalhaes, who teaches worship at Louisville Presbyterian Theological Seminary.

Readers will discover a meditation at the end of each chapter that relates to themes in the chapter. The meditations are sermons I have preached; they show ways that these themes address congregational life in particular settings. My thanks to congregations in Tacoma, Washington; Cary, North Carolina; Shepherdstown, West Virginia; and Lewistown and Ipava, Illinois. Readers can read them in sequence or come back to them later.

I am especially grateful for the wonderful guidance of Beth Gaede, whose editorial skills have greatly improved this work. Mostly, though, my work is made possible by the patient and loving presence of my wife, Jan, who, in her own way, provides a model of nurturing presence in the world, as well as reads drafts of my manuscripts and offers suggestions.

Finally, it is my hope that this book will prompt conversations in congregations and classrooms about the ways that our distinct communities of faith can embody the gospel in the world and point to God's faithful presence.

PART I

Journeying toward Baptism

CHAPTER I

Looking for Water?

ON A WARM, SUNNY DECEMBER morning in Santo Domingo in the Dominican Republic, my son, Andi, and I walk down the street to visit the orphanage where he worked for three months. We stop at the juice vendor's stand for breakfast before turning the corner and heading toward the orphanage compound, several modest cinder-block buildings just two blocks from the ocean. As we walk through the gates, we notice a crowd of people gathered in the courtyard. In one corner a woman stands holding a Bible, preaching fervently to the men, women, and children who have gathered. At the same time, some of the men are filling a large swimming pool in the courtyard with garden hoses that wind around the palm trees. As the water level rises, young men pour buckets of hot water into the pool to warm it up a bit. Finally, the sermon ends, and a band leads the congregation in song. The pool is nearly overflowing, and the minister makes her way toward it and climbs into the chilly water. I discover that I am standing with the group of candidates for baptism, and for just a minute, I wonder if someone will push me toward the pool so that I too will be baptized.

The band jams away, playing old American gospel hymns and singing them in Spanish. One by one, men and women climb into the cool water of the pool to be immersed, taken under the water, and lifted up. Most people are not watching the baptisms, however. They are singing and clapping as young children scamper around the courtyard, waiting for the service to end, so that they can finally share in the community's noon meal. I am riveted by the baptisms, as I watch the pastor whisper in each individual's ear before she lays them back in the water and raises them up.

There are occasional shouts of "Hallelujah!" as family members watch the baptism of a relative or child. Tucked in the corner of the courtyard, I take pictures and sing along in English to these old hymns from my childhood.

Then a young man, wrapped in a towel and still dripping wet, comes over and stands next to me. He greets me in English, and I congratulate him on his baptism. As we sing along together, he turns to me and asks, "How do you know these hymns?" There in the courtyard of an orphanage, far from my seminary office in Richmond, Virginia, I feel connected to this stranger. In that moment I see that we are family. This truth, grounded in Scripture, enacted in water, and expressed in song, becomes clear.

This experience has become central to my reflections on baptism and has prompted me to write this book. I am a middle-aged, white, American, male, Presbyterian minister and seminary professor. Each of these adjectives (and others descriptors that could be added to the list) defines me in a certain way and shapes the way I experience the world. Baptism has the unique possibility of taking us out of our comfort zones and connecting us with others in unfamiliar settings, even in other cultures and countries, even in the most unlikely of places. The truth of the matter is that whether this young man in the Dominican Republic and I would agree on theology, politics, philosophy, or a host of other topics, we stood side by side for a moment sharing an experience that united us. It is this greater truth—the ability of baptism to connect us to one another despite our differences—that provides a needed testimony in a world torn by divisions. The reflections on baptism in this book will inevitably show my own theological and liturgical preferences and biases. However, the primary aim is to encourage congregational leaders, pastors, educators, and active members to reflect on baptism as a part of their lifelong journey of faith. I am exploring baptism here not simply as a moment in time, but as a defining experience and primary metaphor for Christian discipleship.

As one who teaches worship (including classes on baptism) to students from various denominations and ecclesial bodies, I am well aware that baptismal theologies and practices often divide us. Practices are neatly categorized into sprinkling, pouring, immersion, or submersion; infants, children, teenagers, adults. These divisions are repeated in most books on baptism, which reinforce the division between those who practice infant baptism and those who practice believer's baptism. In contrast, we will explore Christian discipleship through the prism of baptismal imagery in Scripture, history, and experience. We will search for unifying patterns of baptismal formation that will guide the choices we make each day. This book follows the individual's journey through baptism, beginning with inquiry, through the preparation for baptism, the event of baptism itself, and a time of discernment following baptism. Recent ecumenical conversations about baptism have uncovered liturgies of the early church and common denominators that point to areas of convergence in baptismal practice and theology common to a number of denominations and ecclesial bodies.

Despite our ecumenical progress in recognizing and affirming one another's baptismal practices, much work remains. It is difficult and risky work, challenging the tight definitions and boundaries of many of our denominations in our approaches to baptism. Yet in this postmodern and increasingly secular time, this work potentially points toward a shared future in which Christian formation, identity, and daily life will unite followers of Jesus Christ despite distinct theological doctrines and beliefs. On this journey, biblical texts and early Christian documents provide glimpses of ways that Christians have struggled with their understanding of baptism, albeit in vastly different contexts and cultures.

Memories

On a chilly, wet January evening, members from neighboring Roman Catholic and Presbyterian parishes gathered for worship. The two church buildings were three blocks apart, and the congregations had a long history of cooperation. In fact, one couple attended services weekly at both churches. They talked about the common use of Scripture each Sunday and similar practices in both congregations. Yet, despite areas of agreement, deep divisions remained. When we gathered annually to celebrate the Week of

Prayer for Christian Unity, we were not able to share the central practice of congregational life—gathering around the Lord's Table to break bread and share a cup of wine. On this occasion, we gathered to remember our baptismal vows—made separately in our respective churches—and to pray for the day when these vows could be shared. During the service we lit candles and walked in procession down the street from one sanctuary to the other. We understood our walk as a public witness: we were carrying the light of Christ through our neighborhood. As we walked and sang, the wind whipped at the flames of our candles, and the raindrops doused them. By the time we arrived for the rest of the service, our candles were out and our clothes were damp. When the group re-assembled for prayer, the minister reminded us of the Spirit's wind that blows through our lives and the rain that falls to sustain the earth and serves as a sign of our baptismal vows. Baptismal renewal was no longer an act inside the walls of the church, defined and controlled by ecclesial rules. Suddenly, the rain that we had walked through took on our baptismal promises.

This vision of baptism that unites Christians was expressed in the work of the Faith and Order Commission of the World Council of Churches. *Baptism, Eucharist and Ministry*, published in 1982, points to the longing of communities of faith to recognize one another's baptismal practices.

> The inability of the churches mutually to recognize their various practices of baptism as sharing in the one baptism, and their actual dividedness in spite of mutual baptismal recognition, have given dramatic visibility to the broken witness of the Church. . . . The need to recover baptismal unity is at the heart of the ecumenical task as it is central for the realization of genuine partnership within the Christian communities.[1]

Recently, some theologians have called for joint baptismal services at times like the Easter Vigil, or for building baptismal spaces to be shared by neighboring congregations. These suggestions seek to live out the hope expressed in the statement by the World Council for an ecumenical witness that testifies to baptism as a unifying act of the church. Equally important is that these proposals seek to eradicate the popular heresy often expressed by congregational members who speak of being baptized as a Methodist, a Lutheran, a Presbyterian, or a Baptist. This notion of parochial baptisms runs contrary to the central claims of the gospel—that baptism is a defining moment of discipleship for a follower of Jesus Christ rather than an act of enrollment in a particular denomination or ecclesial body. Although baptismal identity is associated with the theological accents of particular expressions of Christian faith, the act of baptism is the central witness of the church universal that our commitment to follow in the way of Christ supersedes the historical separations that continue to divide Christians from one another.

It is this perspective of baptism as a common profession of faith in Jesus Christ that undergirds the thesis of this book. Rather than being sidetracked by arguments over baptismal mode, this approach, built on common practices in congregations, demonstrates a consensus that is often obscured by the formal positions of institutions. This approach does not presuppose full agreement in all areas. Instead, it recognizes that even shared rituals can be interpreted and appropriated in distinctive ways. To move in this direction requires a sense of measured modesty—that we step back from the dogmatic claims about baptism trumpeted by many within the church. Then we gain the possibility of seeing our actions in a new light and recognizing what we hold in common with Christian brothers and sisters from other parts of the church and the world.

Beyond the movement for Christian unity, it is equally significant to provide this witness to those outside the church who are often bewildered by the internal debates and bickering within the church. We live in neighborhoods of increasing religious diversity, and baptism can serve as a shared Christian witness. While this acknowledgment will not erase theological distinctions that separate us, it will provide some clarity about our common commitment to follow Jesus Christ. This book is offered as a prayer and a hope that congregations and ecclesial bodies will embrace the practices that unite us more than the doctrinal claims that divide us.

Question Marks

I recently discovered how architecture can present the claims of baptism in a new way. The Church of St. Francis overlooks the lake in a huge public park in Pampulha, Brazil, on the outskirts of the city of Belo Horizonte. This small building was designed by the famous Brazilian architect Oscar Niemeyer. The back wall of the sanctuary is made entirely of glass, so that the congregation looks out on the water—as if to say that the baptismal water cannot be contained inside the church but is connected to the water in the lush park that surrounds the building. The baptismal space inside the sanctuary is even more provocative. Near the glass wall, it forms a question mark. Four bronze panels line the inside of this baptistery and portray the Garden of Eden. In the first panel, Adam and Eve are pictured in the garden, surrounded by the goodness of creation. The adjacent panels picture their temptation by the serpent, their participation in the fall, and their exile from the garden. The artwork suggests that as we step into this space for our own baptism, we share the same fate as Adam and Eve. Surrounded by the goodness of creation (just outside the glass wall of the church), we turn away from God and turn upon one another.

Equally startling are the tile murals that wrap around the outside of this architectural question mark. They portray the story of Jesus's baptism in the Jordan River by John the Baptist. Jesus enters the water as the sky opens and a dove descends upon him as a sign of the Spirit's presence in his life. As the baptismal candidate stands in this space, she is surrounded by a second story—that of participation in the life of Jesus and preparation for ministry and service in the world. That these stories together form a question mark only serves to heighten the image of baptism as a transitional passage in our lives.

Because of this stunning architectural design, I have started thinking about the act of baptism itself as a central, defining question in our lives. In most congregations the baptismal service includes questions that are integral to the act of baptizing. For example, in a Baptist congregation, the pastor stands in the baptistery and asks the baptismal candidate, "Do you trust Jesus as your Lord and Savior?" Similarly, many Roman Catholic and mainline

Protestant congregations have adopted the ancient practice of asking the baptismal candidate (or, if the candidate is an infant or young child, the parents and sponsors) a series of questions known as renunciations.

> Do you renounce the devil and all the forces that defy God?
> Do you renounce the powers of this world that rebel against God?
> Do you renounce the ways of sin that draw you from God?[2]

In some traditions these questions to the candidate are followed by the entire congregation's reciting the Apostles' Creed (widely recognized as the baptismal creed of the ecumenical church), as prompted by a series of questions.[3] Then there is the question in the Presbyterian baptismal service that sometimes sounds whimsical: "Do you desire to be baptized?" The answer seems obvious, and yet it places the basic question before the one who is coming to be baptized.

I want to press this question metaphor even further and to assert that not only this moment of baptism but indeed our whole lives form a perpetual question mark. Longing for God, for wholeness, for spiritual renewal in itself raises questions about one's life and priorities. Preparing for baptism can be pictured as a time of questioning. Studying Scripture and learning about the life of faith require intense questioning. Following Jesus Christ involves constant questioning as we seek guidance and make choices about how to live each day. Thus, I will be exploring baptism as a lifelong journey, as a question mark that hovers over us, constantly prodding us to examine our lives and our relationships with God, with one another, and with the earth that God created.

Most of us are familiar with theological slogans claiming that Jesus is the answer. The gospel is presented as the antidote to all our problems. By contrast, the image of baptism as a question mark supports an understanding of the gospel as a lifelong question. Rather than providing easy answers or dogmatic certainty, the gospel constantly questions our priorities, self-reliance, and actions.

In the Gospel of John, the calling of disciples begins as a question to those who are interested in Jesus's teaching. According to the story, on the day after John the Baptist baptized Jesus, he saw Jesus walking past him and called out, "Look, here is the Lamb of

God!" (John 1:36). Two of John's disciples started following after Jesus, and Jesus turned to them and asked a question: "What are you looking for?" The question posed an existential dilemma for those who moved from following John to following Jesus. Immediately, they had to examine their hopes. I like to imagine the scene as a single cinematic frame. The two men stand frozen in space, in a moment of indecision, between their teacher John and this new one who has come onto the scene. Which way will they turn? Will they go back to join John in the prophetic work he is doing in the wilderness? Or will they venture out in a new direction? The Gospel writer describes their questioning: "'Rabbi' (which translated means Teacher), 'where are you staying?'" (John 1:38). Jesus offers no assurance or certainty but simply a challenge: "Come and see" (v. 39).

Like these first disciples, we face the question the gospel poses us. As a college student, I was shocked and shaken by a small book I read by New Testament scholar Rudolf Bultmann, which posed the question in these words: "What is the importance of the preaching of Jesus and of the preaching of the New Testament as a whole for modern man?"[4] While some found Bultmann's methodology objectionable, he pressed the question that the gospel places over our lives with force and clarity. The purpose of Christian preaching, according to Bultmann, is not to provide doctrines that sound reasonable or to require listeners to suspend their intellectual reasoning. Preaching the gospel addresses humans at an existential level when it questions our own self-reliance and asks us to place our trust in God.[5]

Leading with Questions

Preachers and congregational leaders face different tasks when we read the gospel as a question about our priorities and lives. The task of ministry shifts from providing information, facts, and arguments that persuade people to accept our interpretation of the gospel to sharing the profound (and necessarily troubling) questions that we encounter in the Gospels. These traits are central to the conversation about baptism, because baptism is ultimately related to recognizing and celebrating God's acceptance of us as beloved sons and daughters. Effective leaders underscore the ways baptism fosters growth in the life of faith as a community lives together as followers of Jesus Christ.

CURIOSITY

Effective leaders possess lifelong curiosity. The gospel is a strange and foreign text that we read to discover a word that transforms us. It is easy for pastors, educators, and leaders in the church to become so accustomed to biblical texts that we simply lose any ability to be surprised, let alone challenged. The stories of the Bible can become tame and domesticated, and we often use them in defense of the choices we have made. When we become comfortable with the text, we run the risk that our preaching and teaching become a series of theological clichés. Sermons become predictable, and it is little wonder that congregational members fall asleep and visitors quietly slip out a side door.

To maintain a sense of curiosity about Scripture and the life of faith, leaders must embrace a lifelong approach to learning. It is important to continue reading current theological works and new approaches to biblical interpretation to cultivate an ongoing dialogue with biblical texts. Equally important is active engagement with material outside theological and ecclesial circles. Exploring the arts through film, theater, museums, and other art forms is one important way that congregational leaders can discover new ways to read and interpret biblical texts. The arts hold the capacity of breaking texts open in dramatically new ways and helping us see our biases in a new light.

RESPECT

It is essential that leaders in the church today recognize that they may identify a list of questions to address from the gospel that does not match the questions others see as a priority. Thus, from the start, we must recognize the value of listening to the questions others may ask of us in light of their readings of the gospel.

Respect is also demonstrated when we recognize the various places on life's journey where people find themselves. When I first started serving on a church staff, we developed a Sunday-evening program that offered classes on a variety of topics, including Bible study, church history, and thought-provoking fiction. One group I led worked its way through Robert Pirsig's classic book *Zen and the Art of Motorcycle Maintenance*. As we neared the end of our conversation about this book, a young woman raised her hand and asked, "Why can't the main character in this book simply stop asking himself questions since it seems to constantly agitate him?" At the time, I was so shocked by her question that I could hardly respond. It had never occurred to me that we could shut ourselves off from asking questions about the meaning of life or about what the gospel requires of us. However, as I continue to reflect on her question, I have come to realize that we can live with varying degrees of uncertainty at different times of our lives. I believe that some of this difference is determined by our individual temperaments, while our own life situations may also play a decisive role. Effective leaders need to be able to read specific circumstances that may affect the questions people ask, so that the leaders know when to press questions and when to give people space to reflect on their own. Similarly, in times of significant change or crisis, congregations may have a low tolerance for reflecting on questions. Here, leaders must learn the skill of encouraging individuals or congregations to face the basic questions of the gospel, while allowing people time to absorb and reflect on the claims of the gospel on their lives.

OPENNESS

Closely aligned with the characteristics of curiosity and respect is a spirit of openness in congregational leaders. Like curiosity, a sense of openness encourages discussion, dialogue, and debate as we search for ways to live together in light of our readings of Scripture. Effective leaders long for new insights to help them understand a variety of perspectives. Recently I participated in an annual interfaith service for peace that was first held shortly after the horrible events of September 11, 2001. Now each year leaders and members from many faith communities come together and pray for peace and understanding. In Richmond, I gathered with Hindus, Muslims, Sikhs, Jains, Baha'is, Jews, Buddhists, Zoroastrians, and other people of faith to discuss the ways that the Spirit prompts us to work together for peace. There at our gathering, an eight-year-old Jain girl, Shivani Kundalia, mesmerized us as she told stories from her faith tradition, urged us to learn from one another, and softly chanted a prayer. As she spoke, the words of Jesus came to mind: "Let the little children come to me, and do not stop them; for it to such as these that the kingdom of heaven belongs" (Matt. 19:14).[6] Adopting an openness to others and to new perspectives is one way of living out Jesus's teaching.

Another characteristic of openness is demonstrated by a non-dogmatic approach. The leader comes not as a know-it-all expert but as one who invites and practices reflection on the central questions of faith. For preachers, this approach necessitates a shift from providing solutions to inviting listeners to welcome questions as part of the faith journey. Theologian Paul Tillich commented on doubt as a "necessary element" of faith[7] and wrote about the courage required to embrace faith that includes room for doubt and questioning.

GROUNDEDNESS

A sense of being well grounded functions as a primary way to balance the first traits I discussed. Unfortunately, openness and curiosity can lead to a vapid approach that prompts people to chase after the latest theological novelty. By contrast, strong and effective leaders have a theological basis that allows them to navigate the winds of change. This is different from a fixed, set-in-stone religious certitude. Instead, leaders speak from their own beliefs and values, acknowledging that they do not have all the answers, but expressing a sense of conviction. In describing this approach, the philosopher Ludwig Wittgenstein noted:

> Giving grounds, however, justifying the evidence, comes to an end. But the end is not certain propositions' striking us immediately as true, i.e. it is not a kind of *seeing* on our part; it is our *acting*, which lies at the bottom of the language game.[8]

Here Wittgenstein points out that ultimately our actions provide a witness to our perspectives. Leaders who welcome questions live out their Christian faith in ways that guide their personal lives as well as their congregational duties. This sense of being well-grounded refers to the ways that leaders' faith and lives are carefully integrated.

PASSION

Transformative leadership grows out of a deep sense of passion to participate in the reign of God. A former colleague of mine once remarked that his search for a church home was driven by the hope of finding someone who seemed to deeply believe what he or she was preaching and to care about the consequences of living in light of these convictions. Many congregations, especially mainline Protestant ones, face declining membership, financial challenges, and questions about long-term viability. Leaders who can make a difference in these settings are driven by a deep passion for the good news of Jesus Christ, a strong love for the people in a congregation, and a sense of possibility, hope, and expectation that the Spirit will bring the gift of new life.

A Place to Start

Throughout the history of the church, birth has served as a primary metaphor for baptism. This image, deeply rooted in Scripture, is based on interpretations of John 3. Nicodemus comes to see Jesus by night to learn more about this nascent movement of followers growing up around Jesus. Nicodemus recognizes that Jesus is a teacher and leader (note that he refers to Jesus as "Rabbi") who comes from God and whose signs give witness to God's presence. Jesus's response to Nicodemus's question "How can I inherit eternal life?" is that the ability to see God's reign depends on the new birth that comes about through water and the Spirit.

Birth is identified as a beginning rather than as an end in itself. Our reflections on baptism will underscore this approach by framing the discussion of baptism as an unfolding process of birth and growth. Along the way, we will examine key questions that accompany us on this journey as we look closely at four parts of this journey into Christian faith:

1. Inquiry: *Why* am I here and *where* am I going?
2. Preparation: *When* will I be ready for baptism?
3. Baptism: *To whom* do I belong and *how* will we mark this occasion?
4. Reflection: *What* do I have to offer this community?

With this as our map of the discipleship journey, it is time to move forward to examine the way these questions continue to shape and challenge our lives.

MEDITATION I

Baptismal Ingredients

MATTHEW 3:1–12; ROMANS 15:4–13

Every once in a while my work here at the church takes me to places where I would not normally go. Last Thursday morning, I ventured to a place I had not visited in the past three years: the mall. As I was preparing for the service today, I realized that we needed baptismal towels. At times during the history of the Presbyterian Church, towels were virtually unnecessary, since water was nearly absent from the act of baptism. In fact, a video on baptism produced by our denomination showed a minister dipping his hand into the water, shaking it off, and then placing it on the head of an infant. It looked to me more like a clammy welcome to the club than a sacred ritual of initiation and new beginning. This morning, in keeping with the rubrics of our worship book, water will be visible and audible. For those of you who have been part of baptisms here in recent years, this will come as no surprise. Giffin Lowrie is still unhappy with me for dousing his new suit with water at his baptism on Easter Sunday five years ago. At the Easter Vigil service two years ago, Katie Ayers was pretty much soaked to the skin. Even I am surprised by how much water one can scoop out of a bowl in three handfuls.

This morning, as we gather around this small bowl of water, Olivia and Grace are going to get wet. The reason they will get wet is that in baptism we use water both to claim and to celebrate their presence with us as daughters of God. This is no small claim, and it deserves to be made visible with an act that is bold and memorable. In our Gospel reading today, we hear the story of John the Baptist calling out the words of Isaiah in the wilderness:

"Prepare the way of the Lord, make his paths straight." It would be easy to dismiss this story, if it were simply about the mumbling of one strange man. But Matthew makes it clear that this wilderness event is a very public gathering. "The people of Jerusalem and all Judea were going out to him, and all the region along the Jordan, and they were baptized by him in the river Jordan, confessing their sins" (Matt. 3:5–6).

The experience and memory of this public event offer an example of why baptism is central to Christian faith. It is this act of being called out, of gathering in and around water, of confessing our sins, that helps us live out the prayer of Isaiah: "Prepare the way of the Lord." Whenever the church gathers around this water, whenever we take time to ask God's blessing on our lives, whenever we promise to pray, support, and learn from one another, whenever we scoop up handfuls of water, we join with Isaiah and John in preparing a way for God to work in us and among us.

This morning, we baptize Grace and Olivia not simply for their own well-being. We baptize Grace and Olivia also as a way of reclaiming and renewing our own connection to God. In and through the simple elements of creation—through water, bread, and wine, through the presence and embrace of one another—we discover God weaving our lives together. It is especially the gift of young people and infants who help us recover our sense of the sacredness of all of life.

The poet William Wordsworth urges us to look back to our childhood to recover a sense of presence around us:

> There was a time when meadow, grove, and stream,
> The earth and every common sight,
> To me did seem
> Apparelled in celestial light,
> The glory and the freshness of a dream.[1]

Olivia and Grace, today it is through your eyes that we seek to see the world to discover what God is doing. This morning, we offer our prayers, our encouragement, and our support to you and to your families for the days to come—that you will grow in wisdom and understanding, in knowledge and the fear of the Lord, and in joy, so that you will continue to show us the celestial and heavenly light that shines in us and around us.

Last Thursday, my trip to the mall became a great adventure. It began as a baptismal experience itself. I walked out to my car in a torrential downpour. While I may have muttered the name of the Divine when I could not open my car door, my words did not follow the normal pattern of responses in the rite of baptismal renewal. I eventually made my way to the mall, but simply driving around the mall parking lot disorients me. I missed one ninety-degree turn, and I found myself suddenly headed down an exit lane. Finally, I located the center of fine liturgical merchandise—J. C. Penney. On the third floor, I discovered that the line of towels we normally use had been discontinued. Evidently there are just not enough baptisms these days to make that merchandise line profitable. I considered offering a scriptural word to the salesperson— like "What would it profit a corporation to gain the whole world but fail to provide for the needs of the baptized?" But for once, I managed to show restraint. Carefully I picked out an alternative pattern—white, the color of new beginnings and new life, with an embroidered blue shell, an ancient sign of baptism. I waited in line at the counter while the women in front of me were busy exchanging bath sets and comforters. Finally it was my turn. The saleswoman congratulated me on my selection. I told her that the towels were for a baptismal service at the church. For just a moment, I felt as though I were speaking Farsi. My words sounded completely foreign. The saleswoman breathed deeply, smiled, and went on with business as usual.

In that moment, I realized once again that baptism is not about business as usual. It is about interrupting the way we usually do things. It is about water splashing over our heads and dripping all over us. It is about holding tightly to one another in good times and in hard ones and sharing our love, support, and prayers. It is about learning to speak this increasingly foreign language of faith as disciples of Jesus Christ. It is about welcoming and wrestling with the questions that Christian faith brings into our lives.

On this Sunday I give thanks for Grace and Olivia, daughters of God, and for their presence and witness today that prompt us to prepare the way of the Lord. This morning I offer Paul's prayer for

the church in Rome as our own prayer: "May the God of stead-
fastness and encouragement grant you to live in harmony with
one another, in accordance with Christ Jesus, so that together you
may with one voice glorify the God and Father of our Lord Jesus
Christ" (Rom. 15:5–6). May God's Spirit be present with us and
among us, so that in word and with much water we may share
together this common calling as followers of Jesus Christ and beloved children of God. To God be the glory. Amen.

CHAPTER 2

Inquiry

IN FOURTH-CENTURY EGYPT, a man by the name of Pachomius, born in Thebes, was one of a group of people abducted by roving gangs to be sent down the Nile River to work as slaves for the Roman army. The group was imprisoned in Thebes in preparation for deportation to a work site. When Christians in the city learned of the prisoners' plight, they brought them food and drink. Their generosity prompted Pachomius to inquire who these people were. He was told that they were Christians, who "are merciful to everyone, including strangers."[1] This act of unexpected hospitality led to Pachomius's conversion to Christianity, and he eventually became a leader in the monastic movement.

When the church was in its infancy, Christians were often a persecuted minority. In some locations, congregations met in secrecy out of fear that worshipers would be imprisoned. Remarkably, though, this movement grew. Ancient documents that describe churches' practices give clues to the reason for their growth. From the earliest days, Christian communities were known for their hospitality and care for the poor. Neighbors wondered what caused these Christians to care for widows and orphans, visit the sick, and take food to those in prison. Many noted that women received freedom and leadership roles that were uncommon at the time.

In his analysis of the growth of the early church, Alan Kreider, a Mennonite scholar on church and culture at Oxford University, describes Christians' service to others as a central identifying characteristic in the emergence of this movement. Christians' response to the needs of those around them set them apart and made them both a curiosity and an attraction. Since worship services were often closed to visitors, those wanting to learn more about the

Christian faith were screened before being granted admission to a Christian gathering.

Hippolytus, one of the early church fathers, describes the questioning required simply to gain admission to part of the service and to hear the reading of Scripture.[2] Visitors were brought to the leaders before the service began and were asked what had led them to attend the gathering. Those who brought visitors to the service were asked to testify on their guests' behalf to help the leaders ascertain whether these newcomers were ready to hear Scripture. The newcomers were also questioned about their lives. Were they married? What was their occupation? Were they involved in work regarded as contrary to Christian faith? For example, were they brothel keepers, idol makers, actors, charioteers, gladiators, soldiers who engaged in combat, magistrates, or magicians; or employed in one of a host of other occupations considered off-limits to Christians? Christians made this inquiry to find out whether these newcomers would be able to hear the teachings of Christ and live in light of them.

Those who expressed an interest in learning more about Christian charity and hospitality were brought to church leaders for further instruction about the way to begin the process of baptismal preparation.

Learning Lessons

This examination of those interested in learning about Christian faith became known as the catechumenate. The word *catechumenate* comes from the Greek word *katecheo,* which means "to sound throughout or instruct." In early Christian contexts, it is related to overhearing the gospel as Scripture is read and teaching is provided. This preparation for baptism lasted in some places for as long as three years and included a series of inquiries (called "scrutinies") to determine what progress the individual was making on his or her faith journey. The emphasis was on how individuals' actions gave evidence of what they were learning from the teachings of Jesus. A primary concern was learning to care for the poor, the marginalized, and the imprisoned.

This defining characteristic of the early church is found in some of the oldest surviving manuscripts that describe Christian worship. Second-century Christian apologist Justin Martyr appeals to the Roman authorities: Christians, he argues, present no threat to the Roman Empire and should not be confused with other religious groups. Justin offers a brief description of community life. "The rich among us come to the aid of the poor, and we always stay together."[3] This description provides insight into the diversity within early Christian communities as well as the sense of solidarity. On Sundays, Justin writes, the community gathers for an assembly, which includes the readings of the apostles' memoirs and the prophets. The president then offers words of encouragement (a sermon or homily) and prayer, which is completed with communion. Once the bread and wine with water have been "eucharistized," they are given to those present and sent to those unable to attend. In addition, a collection is taken to provide for those in need. "And he [the president] takes care of the orphans and widows, and those who are needy because of sickness or other cause, and the captives, and the strangers who sojourn amongst us."[4]

Christian witness to serve the poor provided a contrast to cultural practices accepted by much of the society. Justin Martyr's teaching about Christian faith and life highlighted the dangers of three particular addictions: money, sex, and power (with the occult being a fourth concern). Against the constant desire to accumulate wealth, Justin noted that Christians were marked by a commitment to charity and sharing of resources. "We who once took most pleasure in the means of increasing our wealth and property now bring what we have into a common fund and share with everyone in need."[5]

Early Christian faith communities' distinctive way of life was summed up by Octavius, who wrote in a letter to Caecillius, "Beauty of life encourages . . . strangers to join the ranks. . . . We do not preach great things, but we live them."[6] Those interested in the Christian movement were invited and assisted in changing their lives and becoming better people. This process was carried out by Christians' careful modeling of a life based on values different from those of the popular culture. On the margins of society,

Christians lived, loved, and cared for one another and for those in need around them.

Back to the Future

In recent years, beginning with Roman Catholic parishes, some congregations have begun adopting versions of a catechumenate for baptismal preparation. It is important to note changes in the catechumenate made to accommodate contemporary culture that make the practice different from that of the early church. No one is talking these days about turning visitors away from the doors of our churches or creating elaborate screening processes to determine who can sit in the congregation on Sunday mornings! However, it is worth noting the effects of current cultural shifts that churches are experiencing. Mainline Protestant denominations, in particular, are increasingly removed from the centers of power that they occupied through much of the twentieth century. Previously, joining a church was often understood as a part of one's business and social obligation. In addition to the social aspect of church membership, the predominance of infant baptism in many congregations limited theological understandings of baptism to a welcoming rite for newborn infants.[7] Thus, recovering a fuller understanding of baptism requires a careful re-examination of congregational expectations and practices.

Cultural shifts in the past fifty years have increasingly pressed the church to the margins of society. There is little cachet attached to belonging to most churches these days. Even in the Bible Belt, younger generations no longer view church attendance as a cultural expectation, or regard church as an essential venue for meeting people. Ironically, as evangelical congregations have become more a part of the mainstream culture, their distinctive theological claims have become increasingly associated with political perspectives. At a time when the mainline church has the possibility of offering a countercultural witness from the margins of society, it generally lacks the theological resources from which to make such a stand. Many congregations have difficulty in articulating a basic theology grounded in baptism. Recently, I was invited to give a lecture on baptism at another seminary. During our class discussion, a student told the story of her fiancé's decision to be baptized. When the young man asked her what he needed to know or do, she said that she realized that she had no advice to offer him.

Recovering a baptismal theology that provides a clear witness to the world around us begins by clarifying the ways baptismal practice embodies our understanding of discipleship. Congregations can begin this process by asking themselves: What do we have to offer that is distinctive? Or to put it more boldly: What does the gospel offer that cannot be found elsewhere? This starting point is far different from the market-driven programmatic approach favored by many church-growth experts. Rather than focusing on providing activities that people want, this approach begins by pondering what unique or alternative perspectives and experiences the church offers that are grounded in our identity as followers of Jesus Christ. As congregations become clearer about their own identity, they can testify to the ways members encounter God in their lives. This capacity to articulate one's calling, mission, and identity with a distinctive Christian vocabulary is central to the church's task of reclaiming a robust baptismal theology. Baptismal practice expresses basic theological convictions.

The Public Witness of Baptism

Baptism is first and foremost a public event that gives evidence of one's commitment as a disciple of Jesus Christ. The congregation gathers to support, encourage, affirm, and renew a shared commitment to live in light of the gospel's claims on our lives. When one comes for baptism, we as a whole church community reaffirm our identity. Together, we promise to learn, grow, and encourage one another.

The public dimension of baptism is embedded in practices that underscore the claims of baptism. For example, on the eve of an infant baptism in some congregations in Sierra Leone, the oldest woman in the family takes the young child in her arms for a guided tour of the village. She walks down the streets of the town, pointing out significant places to the babe in her arms. "Here is the school where you will go to learn how to read. This is the house of your aunt and uncle who will help take care of you. Watch out for this house, because it is full of danger, and you can lose your way. This is the church where you will be baptized tomorrow and where you will learn the stories of Jesus." Though the young child will not consciously recall this tutorial, it offers a shared way of life, a map by which the family and community hope to orient themselves and the newest member of their family.

This form of public testimony provides a clearer identity of ways that Christian faith guides us in our lives. On this point, the witness of the early church provides essential and compelling help for recovering more robust and faithful ways for baptism to embody our witness to the transformative work of the Spirit in our lives.

1. *Christians witness from the margins of society about the possibility of new life.* This is a key lesson for churches in the twenty-first century. For better and for worse, the church no longer occupies a role at the center of society. While remnants of Christendom persist in the platitudes of politicians running for office and in the desperate desire of some Christians to force so-called Christian values on the population at large, the reality is that the church has receded from its place of cultural power and dominance. This shift (which is viewed as a loss of influence by many who grew up in the church in another era) brings with it the possibility for congregations to reclaim a distinctive voice. In a culture immersed in consumerism and greed, the church offers a different model: life shared together. In an early account of the birth of Christian communities, the book of Acts offers a vivid description of life in the church: "They devoted themselves to the apostles' teaching and fellowship, to the breaking of bread and the prayers" (Acts 2:42).

The identity of this nascent community is clearly grounded in the memory of Jesus's life and ministry. These early followers of Jesus describe life shared together in fellowship in communion (note the author Luke's signature way of describing communion as the breaking of bread) and daily prayer (most likely the Temple prayers in Jerusalem).

2. *Christians stand with and for the poor by offering hospitality and generosity.* "All who believed were together and had all

things in common; they would sell their possessions and goods and distribute the proceeds to all, as any had need" (Acts 2:44–45).

This sketch of shared life pictures distinct ways the community interacts with the society by welcoming newcomers while also responding to the needs of others. While many scholars consider this depiction of the early church in Acts utopian and idealistic, the primary point is that it presents the church's understanding of its own identity as one that exists in the midst of popular culture, while acting responsively with generosity to all who are in need.

3. *Christian faith takes root as our actions conform to the gospel's call to faithful discipleship.* Christian community is marked by its life together. It is not programmatic, offering classes and interest groups for identified niche audiences (an approach guided by contemporary market principles). Instead, all the members of the community participate in regular, distinctive practices that shape their lives.

Day by day, as they spent much time together in the temple, they broke bread at home and ate their food with glad and generous hearts, praising God and having the goodwill of all the people.
—ACTS 2:46–47

Out of these shared experiences comes a core Christian identity that extends goodwill in responding to the basic needs of people. This identity is what the church has to offer, and baptism becomes a visible expression of full commitment to this shared way of life.

Individuals who visit our churches come in hope of hearing good news. This good news addresses people's core questions about their identity and the meaning and purpose of their lives. These basic questions include: "Who am I?" "What am I doing?" and "Where am I going in my life?" Baptism offers the Christian community's response to these questions. Here, our identity as believers provides an alternative witness to the values of individualism, success, and consumption in the society at large.

This vision of a different way of life in the context of community is found in diverse settings. On a green hillside outside the sprawling metropolis of Sao Paolo, Brazil, we meet Sarah, a young woman who grew up in the Presbyterian Church and who serves as a youth worker in a Jesuit community. She is taking us to meet a group of people who have spent the past few years camping out on the underdeveloped land as a part of the struggle of Brazil's poor homeless people to gain access to property. This small group is a part of the Landless Workers' Movement of Brazil (Movimento dos Trabalhadores Rurais Sem Terra, known as the MST). In the past twenty-five years, the MST has helped more than 350,000 families gain land in Brazil, and an additional 180,000 families are waiting for the government to recognize their land claims.[8] Sarah tells us the story of her commitment to the movement as it relates to her Christian faith and identity. Her work with impoverished youth in the favelas is prompted by her understanding of Christian discipleship, grounded in her baptism as a follower of Jesus Christ. Sarah works day after day in the struggle for dignity, decency, and justice for all people. She takes us from shack to shack to meet with families joined together in the hope and struggle for a modest home, a small plot of land to grow crops, and the chance to become a part of a community that lifts people out of poverty and homelessness.

The Landless Workers' Movement is a dramatic example of the Christian practices described in Acts 2. It presents a testimony to a distinctive, shared way of life that places concern for one's neighbor above one's own self-interest. These communities are providing an alternative vision in which neighbors come together for the sake of the common good. Congregations that engage in similar practices of sharing possessions with the poor and providing for those who are in need recognize that our identity as baptized children of God leads us to care for our neighbors and for the earth as God's good creation.

Baptism is an action that demonstrates conversion. Through baptism, the church invites us to turn away from the constant quest for more toward a life lived in service to our neighbors and in solidarity with the poor, the stranger, the outcast, and the forgotten. Clear Christian identity and a call to conversion require us to turn in a new direction. The gospel presents an alternative to the capitalistic, consumer-driven culture of success. Therefore, a Christian identity rooted in the gospel invites and welcomes visitors to explore and to join the church's ongoing process of conversion and transformation, which is rooted in our lifelong journey of discipleship.

Changing Church Culture

As Christian communities embrace the new opportunity of claiming faith in the margins of society around us, we can learn ways to welcome newcomers from the witness of the church in its early centuries. In his analysis of the practice of conversion in the early church, Alan Kreider points to the complex interplay between believing, belonging, and behaving. Faith communities in different contexts placed distinctive emphases on these three central ingredients to Christian faith. In spite of these distinctions, Kreider stresses the way that action (behavior) served as the starting place for newcomers who expressed interest in the Christian community. As noted previously in this chapter, newcomers were required to care for the poor and marginalized to demonstrate their desire to learn more about this life of faith.

When asked why he does not participate in the life of a congregation, the novelist Reynolds Price replied:

> The few times I've gone to church in recent years . . . I'm immediately asked if I will coach the Little League team or give a talk on Wednesday or come to the men's bell-ringing class on Sunday afternoon. Church has become a full-service entertainment facility. It ought to be the place where God lives.[9]

Our preoccupation with programming for interest groups and the ever-present need to support the committee structures of the institutional church have shifted our focus away from the central place of baptism in the life of faith as a journey of witness and service in the world. What would happen if congregations began to return to the ancient practices of baptismal preparation by inviting newcomers to start by serving in the soup kitchen, the homeless shelter, or the prison ministry? While such an approach might be off-putting to those who long for our society to return to the good old days when the church was at the center of cultural power, it carries with it the potential for making a difference in the lives of marginalized individuals in the world around us (which is, after all, central to the gospel's claim on our lives).

A renewed theology of baptism, then, begins by shifting our response to those who are coming to profess faith in Christ and express a desire to be baptized. A new approach to baptismal preparation will not be satisfied with weeks of new members' classes on church history and doctrine from a denominational perspective. It begins with an invitation to serve in what congregations have often labeled as mission and outreach projects. Because this practice represents a radical shift, some congregations have started by catechizing their own members into this new way of being and living as the church so these members can help guide and teach newcomers.

Picturing New Life

When you ask any of the old-timers how new life came to Grace Presbyterian Church, they all point to the same starting place. It began the spring when there was a hole in the roof of the worship space. For years the congregation had been slowly declining. Members had watched the neighborhood around the old church building change as well. Crime had increased, and the old houses surrounding the church were decaying. Many members moved out of the neighborhood to the suburbs, and while some continued to drive into the city for Sunday-morning services, it looked to be only a matter of time until the church would close its doors for good. The congregation had tried adding new services and offering programs. These might work for a while, but they never seemed to last. As the congregation grew smaller and smaller, all members could do was to gather for the regular worship services. When torrential rain came that spring, the roof sprang a leak and threatened their gathering place. So the congregation took the last of the church's endowment to pay a roofer to patch it up.

The roofer said he would start working on the roof during Holy Week and that the sanctuary would be closed. When the congregation's governing body began to plan the Good Friday service, the leaders looked for another place to meet. Given the choices they were facing, their young pastor encouraged them to try something new. They would walk through the neighborhood and read from the Passion story at places where violence in the neighborhood had erupted during the past year. Under darkened skies, a small group of about twenty people met outside the old sanctuary at noon. They looked up to the sky and to the roofing crew pounding nails. Slowly they made their way down the street to the first gathering place. Late in December, a young boy had been killed by gunfire from a drive-by shooting while playing in his living room. The group stopped in front of the house and began to sing, "Were you there when they crucified my Lord?" An elder read of Jesus praying in the Garden of Gethsemane. And then the members moved on to the next stop. In front of a small grocery store, they gathered at the place where an older woman had been robbed. The force of the blow on her head had caused her to fall, and she was injured so badly that she died several weeks later. Quietly the church members sang again, "Were you there when they crucified my Lord?" Tears filled their eyes as the Gospel was read.

After two hours of walking through the neighborhood, they returned to the church. They were tired, but they promised to meet for an Easter service on Sunday morning. When they gathered two days later, the pastor stood up and announced, "This morning, I have asked a few of our members to speak about the service we held on Friday." One by one, they recounted how deeply they were moved by what they had seen and felt as they walked around the neighborhood. Then the pastor spoke again: "We cannot stay inside the walls of this church any longer. This morning we are unlocking the doors of this church, and we are committing ourselves to working for justice in this community. May the Spirit of God breathe new life into us as we go forth. Christ is risen indeed. Alleluia!"

The change did not come about magically. Day after day, some of the members gathered to eat a small meal and to walk around the same streets of the neighborhood. On Fridays, they began serving a meal at the church for homeless people. On Mondays, they worked in the community garden, planting, watering, and weeding. On Wednesday afternoons, they volunteered as tutors in the elementary school. Every Saturday morning, they picked up trash in the schoolyard down the street.

Starting that season of Easter, each Sunday service included reports on the church's involvement in the neighborhood and an open invitation for members to bring friends and neighbors to help with the work. At the end of each Sunday service, worshipers gathered around the baptismal font and prayed for God to strengthen them and bless the work that had begun. Slowly but surely, Grace Presbyterian Church began to grow.[10]

Invitation to New Life

As congregations experience renewal around Jesus's call to serve those who are hungry, thirsty, naked, imprisoned, and forgotten, newcomers are invited to this shared way of life. It is a pattern of living grounded in the early church described in Acts 2. Congregations are defined by members' care for one another, by their hospitality to strangers, and by their willingness to provide for those on the margins of society. These forms of service become the laboratory of discipleship for all who express interest in Christian faith. Thus inquiry begins with service, and one's testimony grows in the midst of those who stand side by side in the soup kitchen, clothing bank, and free medical clinic. This active form of prayer shapes and forms us as the body of Christ. As we work together for justice, Scripture takes on new meaning in our lives. We can relate experiences in our own life to the stories of the early church in Acts. Inquirers find that their service to others is an essential part of the preparation for baptism. Breaking bread together around the communion table becomes connected to serving bread to the hungry.

Are you interested in changing your life? This is the basic question the church should pose to visitors. The inquiry is linked to an open invitation to serve with a community of people who in light of the gospel are working for peace and justice. Leaders recognize that neither congregational cultures nor individuals are easily transformed. In faith, with a sense of hope and expectation, and depending on God's Spirit to breathe new life into our congregations, our lives, and the lives of newcomers, we share this journey together—young and old, male and female, gay and straight, rich and poor, together side by side as apprentices in the school of discipleship. There is no graduation date, for it is a lifelong journey that we share with one another. We live into our baptisms and learn the ways of discipleship. When we fall and stumble, our brothers and sisters help us to our feet and lead us back to the path. This is the water way, the way of baptismal life that we are invited to live and explore as we learn Christian faith together in a community.

MEDITATION 2

Birth Pangs

1 SAMUEL 1:4–20; MARK 13:1–8

I have never been pregnant. I'm sure this does not come as a surprise to you, given my gender, but it does affect the way that I read these birth stories from 1 Samuel and Mark. It is worth noting that these texts, written by men and usually interpreted by men, choose the experience of women to speak about how God's presence breaks into our lives. Birth stories are about the gift, the surprise, and the struggle for new life that is at the center of our faith.

In our reading from Samuel, it is the story of birth in surprising times and places. Hannah is growing sad and old as she watches her rival, Peninnah, give birth to child after child. Hannah longs for a child to care for and to nurture. So Hannah goes to the temple to pray that God will give her a son. Even the priest in the temple sees little hope for her. Eli assumes that this unusual woman has been drinking too much wine and scolds her for even coming to the temple. Hannah's persistence causes Eli finally to recognize her deep desire for God's blessing. Eli pronounces a blessing on her, and Hannah returns to her home, where in due time she conceives and gives birth to Samuel.

This is a story of persistence and desire, of longing and hope. It is a testimony of faithfulness, as Hannah becomes a model for ways we too can experience new birth. It is not simply the story of Samuel's birth long ago. It is the story of new birth in your life and in mine and in the life of this congregation. It is about God surprising us and giving us hope when we have nowhere else to turn.

While birth images are present in our Gospel reading, it moves in a different direction. The thirteenth chapter of the Mark's Gospel is such an unusual chapter that usually we just ignore it. This passage is filled with strange images of wars, earthquakes, and famines. Today's text begins with the destruction of the temple in Jerusalem. Look at these large stones, say the disciples. The stones in the temple are huge: thirty-seven feet long, eighteen feet wide, and twelve feet thick. Jesus declares that these giant stones will be completely overturned. In the midst of this disruptive imagery, we discover that Jesus is not speaking about the end; he is pointing to the beginning. It is about birth pangs and new life emerging in our midst.

That is why we cannot afford to overlook this strange text from Mark. What starts out as an odd comment about a temple in Jerusalem two thousand years ago quickly becomes a parable for our own time and our own lives. This is a text of transformation. It is the story of our struggle to experience new birth. It is about the seismic shifts and the shock waves that ripple through our lives whenever God's Spirit is moving and breaking up the walls that we have built up in our lives.

That is why I stand here today and speak about giving birth. The church through its history, even though dominated by men, has maintained at least some space and vision for feminine images. Leaders in the early church called the church our mother. Baptismal waters were charged with feminine imagery. Listen to the words of the baptismal prayer in our own worship book: "Pour out your Spirit upon us and upon this water, that this font may be your womb of new birth. May all who pass through these waters be delivered from death to life, from bondage to freedom, from sin to righteousness."[1]

Friends, this community of faith is about allowing and trusting God to give us new birth. It is about joining with Hannah in fervent prayer that God's Spirit will bring us new life. It is about shifting our trust from what we can do for ourselves to what God is doing in us and through us. It is about recognizing that, especially in tumultuous times, God is at work making a new beginning among us.

Tony Robinson, a United Church of Christ pastor, wrote an article describing ways that some mainline congregations are finding new life. As we move from a period of civic faith, when we assumed that everyone was Christian, to a time of participating in the practice of transformation, churches are beginning to ask the question: "What is our purpose today?" Robinson responds:

> It is suggested by words and phrases like "Christian formation," "spiritual development," "healing," and "making disciples." All are images of change, of human transformation. At the church I serve, we find ourselves reclaiming such familiar yet strange words and phrases as "dying and rising," "new hearts and new minds," "being born again," "repentance," "new creation," and "conversion." Our business is the transformation and formation of persons and communities in light of the vision and values of the Gospel.[2]

This morning, we gather here to pray for, to experience, and to celebrate the beginnings of the birth pangs. It is a process that marks our journey through the waters of baptism and throughout our lives. It is a birth that disrupts our lives, changes our priorities, and requires careful attention. It is both an exciting and a frightening adventure.

These birth images of both gift and danger are present in the most unusual baptismal font I have ever seen. The Museum of Anthropology in Vancouver, British Columbia, has a font from the Northwest Coast Tsimshian people that dates back to 1886. A standing male figure, looking rather stern and dressed in a long, bluish-grey robe, holds up a black bowl of water. In a notebook near this striking figure, I found these words: "Used as a baptismal font in a church but was removed when children were frightened by it." I believe that the artist who carved this font knew that birth rituals and stories always carry both a sense of danger and a sense of hope. We know that our lives will be different. We know that the gift of new life will change our priorities and demand special attention. And we know that this new birth is our only source of hope. We have tried to make it on our own, but it is only by God's grace that we experience new life.

Today, we celebrate the persistence of Hannah, the disruption of the gospel, and the gift of new life that comes to us from God. May God continue to lead us through the waters of baptism, so that we will grow in faith and discover the birth of Spirit in us and around us. To God be the glory. Amen.

PART II

Preparing for Baptism

CHAPTER 3

Companions

I STARED UP AT THE ROCK mountain towering above me and wondered why I had decided to climb it. Our group was gathered on the mesa below. "If you are going to make it to the top, then you will need instruction and a guide," our leader announced. And so we paired off, two by two, with the experienced climbers among us matched up with the newcomers. "Those of us who have scaled this cliff will show you the way. It is a difficult climb, but you will be able to make it to the top as long as you pay close attention and follow the moves of your partners." With fear and trepidation, we started our ascent up the red sandstone cliffs. As a person with some fear of heights, I tried hard not to look at the steep drop-off below as we shinnied our way around the rocky face of the mountain. I focused on my partner ahead of me, who would point out small toeholds and cracks where I could place a hand. Much to my amazement, step by step we scaled our way to the top of the cliff. As we looked out across the high desert landscape of Ghost Ranch, one of our leaders pulled out a small tin flute and begin to play a haunting, lyrical melody. A giant eagle dropped from the sky nearly to the mountaintop where we sat. In that moment, joy and satisfaction and a sense of accomplishment bubbled up inside me.

We know that we need trainers and coaches to accomplish new and difficult tasks. If we are wise, we are quick to acknowledge (and hire) experienced people, from tour guides to personal fitness trainers, who can help us find our way or learn the ropes. When it comes to Christian faith, though, more often than not we expect people to make it mostly on their own. Part of the problem lies in

how we have come to view Christianity either as private experience or as a matter of intellectual assent. When we view Christian
faith as our own private experience, we tend to approach it with a
kind of super-egalitarianism, thinking, why does anyone else need
to validate or tell me about my feelings? When we think of faith as
a matter of intellectual assent, agreement to a certain list of Christian doctrines is enough to satisfy the questions posed by some
congregations.[1] Faith becomes a form of rational agreement with a
list of doctrines. Either way, an individual is left largely on her own
to navigate this new territory. To be sure, there are services and
classes that provide an essential communal context for people to
talk about "private experiences" or "personal beliefs," but often
inquirers must try independently to develop spiritual disciplines
and learn to integrate faith and life, strange and difficult tasks.

In the preceding chapter, we noted how the early church addressed new Christians' need for mentoring through the use of
sponsors who accompanied those who were inquiring about Christian faith. Sponsors provided an initial welcome to the Christian
community as well as guidance each step of the way. Sponsors testified to the earnestness and diligence of inquirers. In areas of the
ancient world where Christians were at times persecuted, this was
a particularly significant assignment. Granting a newcomer even
limited access to Christian gatherings required the community to
exercise trust that the newcomer would not alert authorities or
others who might bring persecution or risk to the group. From the
very beginning of the process, as sponsors brought visitors to the
gathering, they required inquirers to demonstrate their commitment to learn about the Way—the life of Christian discipleship.
It is especially important to note that sponsors were generally not
those responsible for leadership roles in the community. They were
Christians whose lives gave evidence of the transformative claim
of the gospel.

This central ingredient of leadership by congregational members has been at the forefront of congregations that have renewed
a commitment to baptismal preparation (often known as the
catechumenate). Trained sponsors accompany those engaged in
the process of learning about Christian faith. Clergy may be involved in support roles throughout the process, but the bulk of the

learning occurs as sponsors and catechumens study, work, pray, eat, and learn side by side. Through this process, established congregational members gain fluency in their own faith and serve as real-life examples of Christian faith in action.

For example, learning becomes a collaborative partnership as those who have experience read Scripture with those who may be reading the Bible for the first time. A portrait of such a relationship can be found in Acts 8, which tells of the encounter between Philip and the Ethiopian eunuch. This court official is traveling south after worshiping in Jerusalem. While he is interested in the Jewish faith, Deuteronomic law prohibits him from converting, because of his physical condition. Yet traveling home from his visit to the temple, he is seated in a chariot, reading aloud from a scroll of the book of Isaiah. Philip overhears the man and inquires whether he understands what he is reading. The eunuch responds, "How can I without a guide?" So the eunuch and Philip carry on a conversation about Scripture as they travel together. Philip interprets the text and proclaims the gospel to his companion. When they pass a body of water, the eunuch asks Philip, "What is to prevent me from being baptized?" (Acts 8:36).

In a close examination of this text from Acts, United Methodist minister Dan Benedict identifies a series of movements that lead the Ethiopian eunuch to be baptized. Benedict outlines a seven-step pattern: search, discipleship, journey, discernment, initiation, joy, and transformation.[2] Benedict recommends this pattern as a descriptive (rather than prescriptive) way to deepen baptismal practices in the church today.

As we are discovering, this movement from inquiry toward discipleship requires a companion who can mentor one in ways of growing into a life of faithful discipleship. Perhaps the clearest portrait of this kind of companionship in our society is modeled by 12-step groups. An individual acknowledges a need and desire to change and is welcomed into a gathering. Within a circle of strangers, people begin to speak of their struggles and hopes.

They simply tell their own stories with the candor that anonymity makes possible. They tell where they went wrong and how day by day they are trying to go right. They tell where they find strength and understanding and hope to keep trying. Sometimes one of them will take special responsibility for another—to be available at any hour of the day or night if the need arises. There's not much more to it than that, and it seems to be enough. Healing happens. Miracles are made.

You can't help thinking that something like this is what the Church is meant to be and maybe once was before it got to be Big Business. Sinners Anonymous.[3]

It is this kind of honest, supportive conversation about the challenges and struggles in our lives that a renewed catechumenate employs as we work together to discover faithful ways of following Christ.

Patterns for Leaders

For congregations to embrace this approach to providing mentors requires a shift in leadership style. The image of the minister as the all-knowing expert is replaced by that of leaders who share responsibility with others in the congregations for the task of teaching and guiding newcomers. Many congregations continue to struggle to find a model of companionship that will help sustain and deepen faith. The primary emphasis in this approach is on nurturing and supporting growth in the life of faith. Some congregations have changed their worship styles to foster numerical growth (particularly to reach younger groups of people). Ironically, the shift from traditional to contemporary worship fails to address the deeper need: fostering a community of shared discipleship. It simply provides a substitute form: the praise band takes on the role of the organist, or the expert preacher in the pulpit is replaced by the PowerPoint-assisted motivational speaker.

I am suggesting that rather than pursue the next church-growth formula, congregations ought to focus attention on a life of Christian companionship and on ways that the journey of discipleship, saturated in baptismal imagery, serves as the central focus for congregational ministry and mission. I discovered the formative power of such an approach when I was inspired to start a reading group on the Gospel of Mark.[4] I simply announced that on a coming Tuesday evening, I was going to open my living room to anyone who wanted to join me in reading Mark. No expertise was needed. Twice a month, we gathered to read a brief passage in Mark and were guided by some basic questions: Who are the characters in this story? What is the plotline? Who has power in this text? Where do you find yourself in this story? Our group included those who had spent their lives in church and were quite familiar with the text and those who were hearing it for virtually the first time. No one among us claimed to have all the answers. We were exploring the text together, and, in fact, on occasion we identified with a diverse array of characters in the narrative. There was little interest in figuring out the "right" interpretation, as if only one perspective could be valid. Instead, we explored the text from the widely differing backgrounds that we brought to it. Along the way, remarkable things began to happen in our group. One evening, after many months of wrestling with a variety of stories, a scholarly member of our group who had grown up in the church suddenly blurted out, "I had no idea that Jesus spent so much time with poor people." In this moment of discovery, this individual suddenly found himself being addressed in a new way by the Gospel (and through his discovery, we were all challenged to look at the relationship of Scripture and our own lives). In reflecting on this experience, I discovered some essential elements of faith formation that challenged my assumptions about ministry.

1. *Ministry is about sharing life together.* As we sat in chairs and sofas around a coffee table, we examined the ways Scripture addresses our lives. Together, we wrestled with strange and difficult texts. As pastor, my primary role was to raise questions and reframe insights, rather than to explain the historical background of a passage. The task here is to point out perspectives within texts, which may help us to hear them in new ways. There were times, of course, when the exegetical skills I had learned were invaluable in helping open up space for new perspectives. More often than not, though, my role was to be a fellow sojourner looking for connections to my own life in these sacred texts. Together, we learned from and supported one another through times of crisis. This approach requires risking openness about one's life, which

often stands in contrast to the carefully boundaried ideals of pastoral care manuals.

2. *Experiences of shared learning change the way a minister preaches.* In his classic text *The Witness of Preaching*, Presbyterian minister Tom Long describes the preacher as one who witnesses to the truth she has experienced, rather than as an impersonal, critical scholar who looks down from the pulpit and proclaims the message of a text. The preacher as witness points to the ways the text intersects with our lives. Long pictures the preacher as one coming from the congregation to use his gifts to help guide the congregation in ways of living the gospel.[5]

3. *Ministers and other congregational leaders are not expert disciples; they are fellow travelers along the way.* This is not to diminish the significant tasks of pastoral ministry and the gifts required to carry it out. It does, however, challenge the model of minister as chief executive officer and administrator for the church. Instead of assuming that clergy focus their primary time and energy on the maintenance of the institutional structures of the church, this model of ministry points to the possibility of mutual reliance on the gifts and talents each person brings to the congregation.

Even the word *companion* (which literally means "bread with") points to this new understanding of ministry as sharing bread with others. We welcome all who want to join us on this journey. Those who are experienced know how to help guide those who are just beginning. This vision of mutual dependence offers an important corrective to the tendency to professionalize ministry. The primary purpose here is to create room in our congregations to welcome those who come with questions. In the process, we are discovering that it is more important to provide hospitality and companionship than it is to assume that we know the answers to people's questions about their lives. This kind of hospitality is deeply rooted in the models of the life of the early church that we examined in the previous chapter.

In this new approach to ministry as life shared together, we make room for newcomers to join us as we seek to learn from one another. The model of apprenticeship, where an experienced craftsman shares his knowledge and skills by teaching as he works alongside newcomers, is an apt metaphor to the extent that it points to the development of skills, insight, and wisdom that are handed on in the pursuit of a craft. However, Christian faith is more than the mastery of knowledge or a set of skills. Christian faith is honed by attending to the needs of the sick, the forgotten, and the marginalized around us. In the previous chapter, we gave particular attention to the way Christians in the early church encouraged and taught these practices to newcomers. By sending inquirers alongside experienced Christians to serve those who were poor, hungry, sick, and imprisoned, church leaders linked the acquisition of faith with the development of these practices of caring. While training in doctrine and spiritual practices would come later, the place to start was surprisingly not inside the church, but out in the world addressing issues of injustice and suffering. By cultivating a sensitivity to the poor and marginalized, inquirers learned shared ministry from those with whom they worked. Their primary preparation for baptism was spent in deepening relationships with companions who showed them how to care for those around them. Their growth in faith was marked by their increasing commitment to serve. When the inquirers were brought before the community, their mentors were questioned about the qualities these inquirers had exhibited during this time of learning. "Have they lived good lives when they were catechumens? Have they honored the widows? Have they visited the sick? Have they done every kind of good work?"[6] Thus, the test was to perform (literally, "to go according to the form") acts of charity as a way of growing in compassion and sensitivity. Developing these central marks of Christian faith was the essential characteristic needed to become a part of the community.

Learning Faith from Others

The portrait of baptismal preparation that we are exploring begins with inquiry guided by mentors who are responding to the needs of those around us. The emergence of Christian faith is linked with these forms of service. As these traits of hospitality and compassion grow, we also begin to see the world around us in a new way. Every day we face the pressures of a society infused with the values of consumerism, greed, and self-reliance. Solidarity with the poor and suffering alerts us to the exploitive role of media in our lives. We are constantly bombarded with messages that portray self-images based on success, wealth, fame, popularity, and beauty. To market products that offer us the illusion of these qualities, advertising seeks to manipulate us through the media. We often fall prey to this seductive trap. I find myself wanting to buy the new car that will cause beautiful people to look longingly after me. It is only as we immerse ourselves in another way of life that we can begin to gain a sense of perspective on the values that are really important in our lives.

Several years ago, a group from the congregation where we worshiped took a mission trip to Nicaragua. About ten of us traveled together to a village in the mountains to explore ways to improve life for its residents. The village we visited has a church and a school for children in the first four grades. Modest homes are spread across the surrounding land. The lush green hillsides are ideal for growing coffee plants, and the townspeople earn most of their money this way. We arrived with our luggage and were greeted by all the villagers, who were curious to meet these North American visitors. The pastor gave us the keys to the church, because it was the only building where we could lock up our belongings, all those things that we were convinced we needed to bring with us. The women in our group slept in the church each night. Men were taken to the migrant worker sheds, small wooden buildings with two wooden platforms for sleeping. During the day, we picked coffee beans and visited farmers who were processing the beans. Part of our work was to encourage the use of a new way of processing coffee beans that used less water and would help reduce pollution from the runoff in the local streams. Current practices of cleaning coffee beans release substantial pollutants, turning rivers and streams toxic.

I most clearly remember a few key experiences from this trip. First is the simple life and extraordinary generosity of the Nicaraguan people. These people who had few belongings constantly amazed us with their hospitality and kindness. The deep faith and embodied spirituality exhibited in their daily prayer meetings remain a source of inspiration. Second, I found myself completely free of the usual distractions. No computers, no television, no stores. Even though I had money, there was nowhere to spend it, so I was not tempted to buy things to entertain myself. For a few days, I was totally dependent on other people. I came to accept that my life was in the hands of others who would provide me with meals and point me in the right direction. When we returned to Managua and then flew back to the United States, suddenly we were once again bombarded with ads for products to buy.

It is important to teach and mentor people in ways that help provide the roots for Christian faith to take hold, so that they can turn in a new direction. One goal of serving the needy is to place us in situations that will challenge us to reexamine our commitments and priorities. In this process, change comes when we let go of our old priorities to make room for Christian faith to grow. In a society increasingly concerned with the question "What's in it for me?" Christian communities can model an alternative approach to life. The church invites me to grow beyond my obsession with my own needs and pushes me into places where my concern is directed toward the deep needs of those around me. Along the way, I am invited to examine my life and reorient the choices I make to discover where the truths of Scripture and the needs of the world intersect. This starting point is decidedly different from questions about how I can get ahead in life or how I can assure myself of eternal salvation. (Simply note the pronouns in the way that these goals are framed.) By contrast the gospel presents a portrait of God's incarnation in the world. We discover and encounter Christ in the lives of those around us. Jesus's teaching in Matthew 25 underscores that meeting Christ is the purpose of feeding the hungry, clothing the naked, and visiting the sick and those in prison. We do this not as a noble undertaking so that we can generously provide from our excess to the "least of these" (as the text has been preached from many pulpits). We do these acts to encounter the risen Christ in the lives of those we serve. In a certain way, we share a mutual witness in our exchanges. Motivated by God's generosity and grace to us, we share with those around us. In the process, they represent Christ to us. In this exchange we are challenged to look carefully at our own lives and values. This form of examination is what the early church called "scrutinies." The purpose of these questions was to ascertain whether inquirers were growing into this new way of life. Were they absorbing lessons from their service to the poor? Were they reorienting their priorities? Were they learning from their sponsors about Christian values modeled by these forms of ministry?

Conversion Stories

The tough message about the demands of the gospel upon our lives is balanced by the companionship and immersion in a life of service to those in need. This reorientation is at the heart of conversion as understood by the early church. The church demanded commitment and evidence of a life changed by service to support the expressed desire for baptism. But this conversion process went through significant change during the third and fourth centuries. Three snapshots from church history will illustrate the shifting patterns of invitation and preparation for baptism as the church accommodated Roman culture.

In the third century C.E., a leading aristocrat named Cyprian of Carthage became attracted to the Christian community through his friendship with Caecillanus, a leader in the Christian church. Cyprian was known in high society for his expensive wardrobe and his love of feasts. When he expressed his desire to become a Christian, he encountered the difficult challenge of reconciling his wealthy lifestyle of consumption with the church's call to serve the poor. When he became a catechumen, he sold lands and estates and turned his attention to caring for the poor around him. According to Alan Kreider:

> His struggle was not to believe what the Christians believed; rather, it was to live as they taught—and as many of them seem to have lived. Cyprian, encountering a community in which "thrift" and "ordinary and simple clothing" were normal, found that luxury was bred into his bones. . . . He was, to use our language, addicted to wealth and power.
>
> But as a catechumen on the road to membership in the Christian church, Cyprian was among people who were learning to live differently.[7]

Cyprian persevered in learning this new way of life, eventually becoming a bishop for the Christian community in Carthage, where
he practiced hospitality by welcoming the poor into his home and
living simply until his martyrdom in 258 C.E.[8]

Such signs of growth provided evidence that inquirers were prepared to learn more about the content of Christian faith. In the
weeks leading up to the time of baptism, inquirers learned the
basics—the Lord's Prayer and the Apostles' Creed. This content,
though minimal, prepared them to participate in the baptismal service. It also anchored the work of reorienting their behaviors and
values—the primary focus of those preparing for baptism. Records
from the third and fourth century make clear that the significance
of this process of conversion was recognized by those both within
and outside the church. When Constantine recognized Christianity
as an official religion in the Edict of Milan in 313 C.E., the church
rapidly took on a public role in Roman society. Documents show
that amid these changes, many newcomers to the church were wary
about accepting the claims of the gospel on their lives. While interested in this new religion, many delayed their baptism because of
an unwillingness to make the required changes. Constantine himself delayed receiving baptism for more than two decades because
of an unwillingness to give up his wealth, power, and privilege.[9]

By the fifth century, the process of conversion had shifted once
more. Volusian, an aristocratic Roman citizen, expressed an interest in Christianity. When he raised questions about the Christian faith, Christians in Carthage forwarded his concerns to Augustine in Hippo. This led to correspondence between Volusian
and Augustine about the demands of Christian faith. Augustine
responded to Volusian's questions by discussing "the reasonable-
ness of Christian faith" and noted that the call to change referred
to "interior dispositions of the heart."[10] Augustine believed that
Christianity supported the authority of the Roman state and con-
cluded, "For someone 'as distinguished and excellent' as Volusian,
conversion would not require a fundamental change in aristocratic
behavior."[11] In spite of these assurances, Volusian was reluctant to
convert to Christianity. Only late in life, fearing the threat of eternal damnation, did he request baptism, which he received shortly
before his death. Kreider says:

At no point did anyone query his social priorities or invite him to change his behavior in light of Cyprian's criterion—the "example of living in Christ" (Ad Quirinuum 3.39). In this Volusian's experience was typical. As Rita Lizzi has pointed out, "In order to encourage the conversion of the wealthier citizens, the bishops modulated their preaching, dealing in an appropriate fashion with the topics of wealth and almsgiving."[12]

These three examples of conversion to the Christian faith by wealthy Roman citizens show the shifting patterns of reorientation and mentoring in the church. As the church became a dominant cultural institution, the demand for inquirers to adopt practices of caring for the poor receded. This central identifying mark of the Christian church was gradually replaced by the expectation that converts would adopt specific Christian beliefs and explanations of Christian doctrine. Baptismal preparation shifted from practices of hospitality and care to acceptance of key Christian concepts. Along the way, the role of sponsors as companions was increasingly replaced by the teaching of clergy and other church leaders.

Reclaiming Practices

Until recently, Christianity held its position as a culturally dominant religion throughout much of the Western world and particularly in the United States. While vestiges of this status remain, the church finds itself increasingly at the margins of society. Some Christian groups continue to press to regain a culturally dominant position, but it seems unlikely, given the increasing religious diversity of most urban areas in the United States, that people in this country will embrace the nostalgic notion that preferential treatment should be given to Christians.[13] The church now has the opportunity to become accustomed to its new place by reclaiming the central values and practices of its identity. The conversion stories we read from the time of the emergence of the Roman church in the third through fifth centuries show how Christian formation practices changed as the church moved from the margins to the center of society. As the church became a part of the society, the demand to change practices and lifestyles slowly weakened. For us, the question is whether we can trace these patterns in reverse as we move from the center to the margins. A renewed emphasis on mentoring and service to the poor as central ingredients in the formation of Christian faith can reinvigorate congregational life. This approach will reinstate the demands of discipleship by pointing us away from ourselves to address the needs of those around us.

A word of caution seems in order: it is unlikely that congregations that reclaim a vibrant model of discipleship will achieve rapid growth or be seen as successful by society's current standards. As we have seen from the previous stories, the church's desire to achieve success by including the wealthy and powerful aristocrats from Roman society influenced the shift in conversion practices. The hunger for success and power by church leaders eroded the basic practices of caring for the unfortunate and neglected— practices that had been central to Christian identity throughout the early centuries of the church's existence. However, I do believe that reclaiming this vision of baptismal formation and discipleship led by sponsors and linked to service to the poor will reinvigorate the church by reestablishing a basic commitment to care for the world and for those in need. The powerful model of providing companions who teach and serve alongside newcomers parallels the portrait of Jesus's ministry in the Gospels: "Follow me, and I will make you fish for people" (Matt. 4:19). Jesus's invitation to discipleship connects with his own life of service to the poor, the marginalized, the sick, the demonic, and the neglected. Service alongside others undergirds the central practice of shared life within a community that invests its time, energy, and money in responding to the needs of those around us. Growing into these practices, which run contrary to the consumerism and materialistic values of the dominant culture, requires dedication and support. These practices provide the church with a powerful witness to the surrounding culture.

Pastors, educators, and other congregational leaders can transform our expectations and experiences of church by helping congregations recover ancient patterns of training disciples in the way of Jesus Christ. On this journey together, leadership will have less to do with providing expertise and more to do with nurturing and sustaining mentors as they embody Christian faith. Ministry will change focus from the dominant model of pastor as professional to a model of shared ministry undergirded by the unique gifts each member brings. While the practice of companionship challenges the authority model of ministry based on one or a few central leaders, it offers ministry as a service of mutual friends and companions who share life together. Mentoring disciples is a long process that rests on the foundation of baptism as a lifelong journey.

Dirty Water, Dusty Feet

2 Kings 5:1–14; Luke 10:1–11, 16–20

In a bookstore in Scotland, I discovered a small book titled *Why People Went to Church,* part of a series on the history of Scotland. Its purpose was to explain why there are so many church buildings in Scotland when so few people actually attend church these days. Both Edinburgh and Glasgow are filled with church buildings, now converted for use by community or civic groups. This phenomenon is common across the European continent, which once was the center of Christendom. In the Pacific Northwest, we are rapidly moving in the same direction. In our own neighborhood, the great mainline Protestant congregations that once encircled Wright Park are all working feverishly for survival and renewal. Not so long ago, most of these churches were comfortably full most of the year.

These days, all of us struggle to meet standards of success from the past. While there may be a few success stories of rapid church growth in the suburbs, by and large, most of our neighbors do not go to church. In a relatively short period of time, the church has gone from the center of society to a place of irrelevance. Presbyterians are the perfect example. In the past thirty years, membership nationally has decreased by nearly 50 percent. No matter how many programs are started or what interest groups happen to control the agenda, the decline continues. But as long as contributions continue, many of our leaders simply continue to reinvent themselves to address the issues of the day. In the span of my adult lifetime, I have watched the Presbyterian Church largely abandon its prophetic voice on issues of peace and justice and increasingly cater to those on the far right who often use finances as a form of blackmail.

Amid all this decline, the changing role of the church is largely forgotten. In many ways, Immanuel is the perfect example of the changes taking place around us. In the 1940s and '50s, most people belonged to a church. It was expected and was part of one's civic responsibility. Churches responded by recognizing and paying tribute to civic institutions. I was reared in small churches where we were more likely to celebrate civic holidays than religious ones. When I was growing up, the Fourth of July was much more important to our congregational identity than Pentecost was. Upholding American values took precedence over growing in our spirituality.

In the past few decades, though, we have witnessed another incredible shift. These days, few people attend church out of a sense of civic or community duty. People come to church out of a desire for relationships and as a part of their search for meaning. Congregations that survive these tumultuous times learn to let go of past expectations and to reach out to those who long for a place of hospitality and hope. Our readings today offer two contrasting but complementary models for the way in which communities address the needs of those around them.

Our reading from 2 Kings is about a stranger who hears about a community of faith and comes in search of healing. Naaman is a commander in a foreign army. He suffers from leprosy, a common term for a variety of deadly skin diseases. In fact, we know from other texts that leprosy was so contagious and so feared that those who contracted this disease were often forced to live in leper colonies, small gatherings of poor outcasts. Naaman is filled with fear for his future. One of Naaman's servants knows of a source of healing. If only Naaman were in Samaria, then the prophet Elisha could cure him, she remarks to her mistress.

By this time, Naaman is ready to try any remedy. Naaman gets a letter of recommendation and a large bag of presents from his king and rides off in search of the prophet Elisha. When Naaman rides up to Elisha's house, Elisha sends out his messenger to point the way to the community pool—the River Jordan. Now Naaman expects far more than this. After all, he is a man of honor and prestige. He expects special treatment—the wave of the prophet's hand and an instant cure. He does not need to go to the dirty water of the Jordan.

Even though it was not the cleanest water, the Jordan River held a special place in the hearts and minds of faithful Jews. The river marked the entrance into the Promised Land for the Hebrew slaves after their long journey through the wilderness. There they began a journey toward a new way of life together. Last week, we read of the Jordan as the place where Elijah and Elisha reenacted Moses's parting of the Red Sea as the Hebrew people left Egypt. For Elisha, the Jordan River serves as a confirmation of his call as a prophet who follows in the path of Elijah. The dirty water of the Jordan River is a source of identity and healing for these people of faith.

Finally, one of Naaman's servants persuades him that, as preposterous as it sounds, maybe bathing in the Jordan River is worth a shot. After all, what does he have to lose? So the great commander of the army of Aram gets down off his high horse, dips himself in the Jordan seven times—and experiences the healing grace of God.

Friends, each Sunday we gather here around this small bowl of tap water. It is not the baptismal font that I still long for as a sign of the significance of our baptism, but nevertheless it is the place where we come to confess our sin and to receive the gift of God's forgiveness. This water unites us with the gift of all creation and the beauty of the world that God gives us. This water takes us back to our true identities as children of God who are made in God's own image. As you and I live out this identity, as we practice our faith, as we speak out and point to the source of our healing, then others will come to experience and share in this place of community. It is this hunger for healing and renewal, for acceptance and care, that this church—and every church—is called to lift up. It is not our job to change the world. It is not our job to tell people what to believe. It is enough to raise our voices and to point to the One who brings us through this dirty water and who weaves our lives together in this community.

In our Gospel reading, Jesus sends out seventy of his followers to the surrounding villages. In light of the recent rejections of Jesus by the neighboring towns, the task is a difficult and dangerous one. Jesus sends them out two by two for security and support.

Their assignment is basic. They are to bring greetings of peace to those whom they meet. They are to share meals and build relationships around the table. They are there to point to the source of healing and to proclaim the presence of God within them and around them. Much to their surprise, the disciples return full of joy and excitement about the Spirit's movement among them.

Friends, it will be the same for us and for this community of faith, as we go out and bring words of healing, as we break bread with our neighbors, and as we point to the source of healing and hope that we experience in Jesus Christ. We do not need church-growth programs and manuals. We need to live faithfully, to work for peace, and to speak of God's grace that reaches out to all people.

Dirty water and dusty feet: these are signs of life for communities of faith. In the midst of great change in our culture and in the life of the church, these signs point us toward the center of faith and lead us to live as followers of Jesus. Through this dirty water, we rediscover our identity and recognize that our source of healing and hope is God alone. And with dusty feet, we work together for the transformation of our world by bringing words of peace to our neighbors. Along the way, we will find the Spirit bringing us together and creating new relationships that will feed and nourish us.

In the movie *The Man Who Cried* (2000) there is a wonderful scene in which a young Russian Jewish woman searching for her identity visits a gypsy camp on the outskirts of Paris shortly before the Nazis make their way to France. In this time of danger, she is greeted by all and offered the gift of music. The old men in the camp take turns playing and singing for her. Then they grow silent and wait for her to offer a song in return. She slowly begins to sing a song of prayer she learned as a schoolgirl in England:

> *When I am laid, am laid in earth,*
> *May my wrongs create*
> *No trouble, no trouble in thy breast.*
> *Remember me, remember me,*
> *But, ah, forget my fate!* [1]

As she sings this ancient song of lament, the gypsies break into a soulful accompaniment, and this mournful song becomes an occasion of joy. As they sing and play, rain begins to fall on them all as a blessing from heaven.

As we offer hospitality to those who come our way, and as we bring words of peace to our neighbors, we will discover new ways of singing and praying together. Let us not grow weary in doing what is right, but whenever we have an opportunity, let us work for the good of all. In the process, we will be writing our own book on "Why We Go to Church." To God be the glory. Amen.

CHAPTER 4

Renunciation

AMY SLIPPED INTO THE BACK row of the sanctuary for the regular Sunday worship service. She was going through a difficult time of transition. A long-term relationship had just ended, and she had received news that her mother had been diagnosed with cancer. She felt as though her world was starting to come apart. She had visited churches occasionally as a child but had never spent much time there. A co-worker and friend had invited her to come to the service and to lunch afterward. To Amy, the entire service seemed strange—new music, long readings from the Bible, unusual rituals. Despite the foreignness of it all, however, something in the service moved her. Maybe it was the feeling of community she sensed in the people around her; maybe it was the warm welcome she experienced from people who reached out to greet her; maybe it was the passion of the preacher as she spoke about her own struggle to understand how to live in light of the gospel. It was just enough to bring her back the next Sunday.

After a few Sundays of watching and listening, Amy decided to do something. She volunteered to help make sandwiches for the homeless meal on a Saturday morning. As a teenager, Amy had run away from home; she still remembered how it felt to be lonely, lost, and hungry. So she began helping out in the kitchen on Saturday mornings. Several regulars from the church befriended her, and she found herself slowly but surely growing into the rhythms of this community. Amy was still skeptical about a lot of what she heard that Christians believe. Finally, she decided to talk to the pastor about her doubts, concerns, and questions. In the first conversation, she found more reassurance than answers. She decided to stick with it for a while because, as she put it, "At least it gave me a group of people who welcomed me and something worthwhile to do on Saturday mornings."

Over time, though, she began to realize that this group was more than just another volunteer organization. She started attending a Bible study on Tuesday nights and began meeting with a sponsor regularly to learn about baptism. While she was learning to depend on this community and its practices, she also realized that she was being asked to move in new directions and to give up old habits. Her regular trips to the mall to buy shoes diminished. When she went out with friends on Saturday night, she came home earlier to make sure she could get up in time for church the next morning.

Getting Ready for Baptism

We have been examining the characteristics and values of a community that attracts individuals and guides them toward baptism. We have given particular attention to hospitality and care for the poor as biblical and historical markers of Christian identity. Inviting and welcoming inquirers into the Christian community requires providing mentors to guide people into the community's way of living the gospel. As newcomers learn positive virtues by serving the marginalized, they are sustained by the worship life of the community that gathers around Scripture to reflect continually on the call to discipleship. Studying and reflecting on biblical texts offers us the opportunity to discover ourselves in these ancient narratives. In this process, we find our identity as children of God who are called to a life of service. This model is incarnational; it looks to the Gospel stories of Jesus's ministry as the primary paradigm. It establishes its priorities by paying careful attention to Jesus's actions and the descriptions of the early Christian communities. We gather regularly around Word, water, bread, and wine to experience the claims of the gospel on our lives. Around Scripture and sacrament, a community forms that leads us beyond our own personal interests. We begin to embody the gospel. We become signs of Christ to one another and for the world.

Preparation for baptism is guided by the desire to become a part of a community that welcomes strangers and gives its life in service to the world. Baptismal preparation is about discovering ways to make these values part of our lives. As one moves toward baptism, he or she also experiences the need to move away from other values. Within the baptismal liturgy, this movement is underscored by a series of questions known as the Renunciation.

Trusting in the gracious mercy of God,
Do you turn from the ways of sin
And renounce evil and its power in the world?

Do you turn to Jesus Christ
And accept him as your Lord and Savior,
Trusting in his grace and love?

Will you be Christ's faithful disciple,
Obeying his Word and showing his love?[1]

A form of these questions was a part of baptismal rites beginning in the second and third centuries,[2] and they now appear in the baptismal rites of most denominations' worship books.[3] Their place in the liturgy marks a transitional moment when the baptismal candidate moves from stating his or her desire for baptism to the act of joining the congregation in professing faith (usually in the words of the Apostles' Creed, recognized by many Christians as the baptismal creed of the church). While some ecclesial bodies (particularly Roman Catholic and Episcopal congregations) continue the historic practice of exorcism that often accompanied these questions,[4] others continue to struggle to interpret them for people in the twenty-first century. Here, the key is primarily to determine what controls our values and priorities.

Amy's search for community and meaning underscores the delicate balance churches face as they provide welcome and acceptance as well as uphold core convictions. Amy wrestled with the strange language of the questions she would be asked as a part of a baptismal service. We might grapple with them, too. What does it mean to "reject Satan and all his works and all his empty promises"?[5] Is that the same as being asked to "turn away from everything that separates you from the love of God?"[6] The formulations of these questions with their distinctive theological nuances do matter. The ways we speak about God and evil provide insight into how we view the world. Here, though, I am primarily interested in exploring the act of renouncing evil as the final preparatory movement in the baptismal rite and its implications in our lives.

Baptism requires that we change, that we leave behind other commitments. Throughout the history of the church, baptism has been understood as a rite of initiation. It is a way of showing a change of status in the community for those who are baptized. The renunciations find their place in this threshold moment.[7] The questions articulate the deep truth that to pledge one's allegiance to God requires one to turn in a new direction. In the early church, the baptismal candidates often embodied the language by turning their bodies to face in a new direction as they answered the questions. Understanding what the renunciations are asking requires careful attention to the entire framework of the baptismal journey. There are several key factors to consider:

1. *The renunciations are present-tense statements.* They ask those who are growing in faith to recognize and acknowledge the choice to turn in a new direction. Renunciation is hard work and an ongoing process for those striving to live into their baptismal vows, however. Within an understanding of baptism as an ongoing journey, our answers do not suggest that renunciation is already accomplished. Renouncing evil and its power in the world is a lifelong struggle.

2. *Like baptism, renunciation is not primarily concerned with rational decisions.* We cannot think our way into turning from evil. Baptism and renunciations require trust as we step forward in faith in a new direction. The language of the baptismal rite from Common Order is particularly instructive:

In this sacrament,
The love of God is offered to each one of us.
Though we cannot understand or explain it,
We are called to accept that love
With the openness and trust of a child.[8]

3. *While the questions of renunciation are addressed to individuals, the individuals are surrounded by a community that promises to support and uphold them on a journey together.* Covenant language often surrounds the renunciation as a way of underscoring a shared commitment to rejecting evil and sin.

4. *Renunciations depend upon the community of faith and the values it teaches to disciples of Jesus Christ.* Rejecting sin and evil is an abstract notion that comes to life in particular contexts.

5. *While baptism is a rite of initiation, the renunciations are not a form of hazing that one undergoes to join the group.* Rather they are a prophetic truth-telling that shows how a life of discipleship requires a different orientation of one's priorities. We turn from the past and from our attachments to society's habits and values, and we turn toward Christ to move in a new direction with this baptismal family.

Searching for Clarity

Amy, our baptismal candidate, wanted answers. She wanted to know what she was being asked to turn away from. She could make no sense of the popular imagery of Satan as the personification of evil lurking around every corner and seeking to entrap people and gain control over their souls. At the same time, Amy recognized the struggle of many around her who battled addictions and seemed perpetually caught in acts of self-destruction. Her experience working in the corporate world and seeing firsthand the insatiable desire for profit and greed at all costs prompted the spiritual search that had led her to visit churches in hope of finding a different compass for her life. These past few months of worshiping regularly and serving lunch to the homeless had caused her to examine her life. Sitting around a table and sharing sandwiches with homeless people on Saturday mornings caused her to consider more closely where she went to eat the rest of the week. Slowly but surely, as she heard Scripture read and proclaimed, she grew in her awareness of the struggle to adopt a way of life consistent with the gospel.

Her struggle came to a climax on the Sunday when the pastor preached on the rich young ruler who visited Jesus. According to Mark, this man ran up and knelt in front of Jesus and implored him, "Good Teacher, what must I do to inherit eternal life?" (Mark 10:17). Jesus responded to the question by pointing to the importance of following the commandments, and the man answered that he had kept all of the commandments since his youth. Jesus replied, "You lack one thing; go, sell what you own, and give the money to the poor, and you will have treasure in heaven; then come, follow me" (vs. 21). The man turned away in sorrow. The message of this text is stark: following Jesus requires us to leave behind exploitive practices that have led to success and wealth. In reflecting on this passage, biblical scholar Ched Meyers notes, "Jesus is not inviting this man to change his attitude toward his wealth, or to treat his servants better, or to reform his personal life. He is asserting a precondition for his discipleship: economic restitution."[9] Amy heard this text as challenging the way she had framed her life and urging her to move in a new direction.

The role of the renunciations is to articulate the church's theology and practice as inquirers engage in ministry to those on the margins of society. The challenge to turn from evil and its power is directly connected to the vision of communal life embodied by the congregation. In earlier chapters we noted that mentors teach inquirers faith as they serve alongside one another. The primary purpose is to reinforce the virtues of hospitality and service to the poor as primary marks of the Christian assembly. These ideals stand in stark contrast to our culture's predominant values of consumerism, materialism, and individualism. Images of success, power, fame, and wealth constantly bombard us through various forms of advertising and media. Christian communities must learn that they cannot compete with cultural norms without sacrificing the gospel message. With the demise of Christendom, the church has moved from the center of society to the outskirts. Our desperate attempts to appear affluent and successful will inevitably be dwarfed by the portraits of wealth and expectations of success portrayed in popular media. In contrast to the endless pressure of upward mobility, an embodied baptismal theology points us in a new direction. The incarnational language of the gospel is particularly instructive. Note how the hymn to Christ in Philippians 2 describes Jesus as the one who "emptied himself, taking the form of a slave" (Phil. 2:7). The renunciations not only become a turning point for those who are coming to baptism; they also remind the church to seek life by turning away from the power of sin and evil.

In his classic children's book *The Wretched Stone,* Chris Van Allsburg provides a morality tale about the dangers of obsession with the notions of success that capture our minds. Shipmates long at sea and bored find a stone box that entertains them with images that flicker across the face of the stone. What begins as an amusing pastime quickly takes over the work schedule as the shipmates begin to spend more and more time staring at the images on the box. Their work habits deteriorate, and they begin to fight with one another over who gets to watch the box. In the end, the captain of the ship is forced to throw the stone box overboard to save the ship and its crew.[10] This cautionary tale shows how powerfully we can become enthralled with images that disorient us. We lose sight of our vocation to care for one another. Only when we turn away from the seductive power that enslaves our imagination and toward Christ do we find an alternative vision of communal life.

The baptismal liturgy presents the demands of this new way of life. The renunciations press us to turn from sin and evil and to rely on God's grace. Biblical imagery associated with baptism portrays different ways to respond. The initial portrait of baptism in the Gospels is that of John the Baptist. John is out in the wilderness, far removed from the centers of political and religious power in Jerusalem. He preaches a gospel of renunciation. Repent, turn around; the reign of God is at hand. His strategy is to attack supporters of the status quo for their preoccupation with religious rules and their sense of entitlement. This call to repentance sees baptism as an act of religious renewal. Jesus joins the crowds flocking to the wilderness to participate in this act of cleansing. For John, baptism by water is preparation for the impending reign of God. Judgment language permeates the message. John offers a harsh warning that the present way is doomed. Like the captain of the ship with the wretched stone box, John believes that the only hope lies in taking drastic action. Baptism in the Jordan River represents the dramatic shift required to prepare us for the coming of God's kingdom.

In the synoptic Gospels, baptism as an act of renunciation is directly linked to Jesus's temptations in the wilderness. The questions of renunciation draw primarily on the temptation story and its portrait of Jesus's struggle with the devil. Jesus is presented with the options to feed himself, to lead a religious spectacle, and to take up a seat of power. He responds by renouncing the devil: "Away with you, Satan!" (Matt. 4:10). In the Gospels these events mark the transition to Jesus's public ministry. Turning away from the call to self-nourishment, fame, and idolatry propels Jesus into a ministry of feeding, teaching, and healing. Many scholars note the parallels between the temptations and the Deuteronomic stories of tests faced by the children of Israel in their wilderness wanderings. Leaders in the early church drew on Old Testament narratives to develop the baptismal liturgy. In Matthew's Gospel the temptations provide an opportunity for Jesus to demonstrate his reliance on God to provide a way into the future. For baptismal candidates, the renunciations provide a formal acknowledgment of their willingness to turn from the past and to devote themselves to a life of service.[11]

The ritual actions of renunciation and baptism do not produce instantaneous change. As Christian ethicist Gordon Mikoski notes, "The revolutionary transformation in inner life and outer behavior does not come as a magical event."[12] Rather, these actions mark the baptismal candidate and place him or her in the middle of the community's life to continue formation as a disciple of Jesus Christ. This vision of baptism as lifelong discipleship that repeats Jesus's incarnation is presented by the apostle Paul. Paul depicts the act of renunciation as a break with the past. Baptism is an act whereby our lives are absorbed into the life of Christ. Here the imagery is that of dying to the old life: "Do you not know that all of us who have been baptized into Christ Jesus were baptized into his death?" (Rom. 6:3). This striking theological claim portrays baptism as a way of participating in Jesus's death and resurrection. According to New Testament scholar C. K. Barrett, "[Paul] has taken a rite used previously in the simple sense of entry into and participation in the Christian fellowship and attached it explicitly to the death and resurrection of Jesus."[13] Purity rites are replaced with a theological claim that participants are absorbed into the gospel narrative in the event of baptism. From this perspective, the primary metaphor of death dramatizes the claim that the baptismal candidate is breaking from the past in order to depend on God's promise of new life in Christ. This radical picture is highlighted in communities where the baptized is given a new Christian name. Here, even one's birth identity is preempted by the adoption of a new name and identity rooted in the biblical narrative.

Renunciation as death to the past draws on the Christian hope of resurrection as the gift of new life. "Therefore we have been buried with him by baptism into death, so that, just as Christ was raised from the dead by the glory of the Father, so we too might walk in newness of life" (Rom. 6:4). Renunciation and baptism come together as a recapitulation of the life, death, and resurrection of Jesus Christ. The liturgy becomes a way of living out the gospel story with our voices and bodies.

The historical development of the celebration of Easter further solidified the identification of renunciation and baptism with Christ's death and resurrection. The earliest celebrations of Easter by Jewish Christians grew out of the historical connections to the Passover calendar. The Passover celebration recalled the Exodus narrative, which was remembered alongside the memories of Jesus's death and resurrection. Central to the Passover celebration was the recalling of the Exodus 12 narrative of the Hebrew people's deliverance from Egypt. The story of struggle for liberation from slavery culminates in the people passing through the divided waters of the Red Sea. Renunciation is linked with emancipation from slavery and leaving the past behind on a journey together toward the Promised Land. Moses negotiates with Pharaoh to gain freedom for the Hebrew people. Pharaoh finally relents, and the Hebrew people begin their journey from Egypt, but they immediately face danger when Pharaoh changes his mind and sends his army in pursuit. In fear and uncertainty, the people cry out to Moses, "We were better off in Egypt as slaves than we are now." Moses's encouragement to trust in God's protection prompts the people to move forward through the divided waters of the Red Sea—toward freedom.

In the early Christian celebrations of Passover, two major themes quickly became woven together through liturgical practice: the Hebrews' deliverance from slavery by passing through the Red Sea and Jesus's death and resurrection. This practice reinforced typological interpretations of Old Testament passages associated with baptism. In his letter to the church in Corinth, Paul recasts the Exodus narrative as a baptismal story where "all passed through the sea, and all were baptized into Moses in the cloud and in the sea" (1 Cor. 10:1–2). Paul adds a christological twist to the account by linking the wilderness-wandering story of the water that comes from the rock (Exod. 17) with Christ: "For they drank from the spiritual rock that followed them, and the rock was Christ" (1 Cor. 10:4). The development of loose associations between major Old Testament narratives and baptism reinforced the archetypal interpretations of baptism as an act of renunciation of the past.[14]

Similarly, the author of 1 Peter appropriates the story of Noah's ark and the great flood as a parallel to baptism. Noah and those in the ark were saved from the waters of the flood, "And baptism, which this prefigured, now saves you—not as a removal of dirt from the body, but as an appeal to God for a good conscience, through the resurrection of Jesus Christ" (1 Pet. 3:21).

By the second century, most church leaders showed a preference for baptisms to take place during the celebration of Easter. At the end of the second century, Tertullian recommended Easter as a primary time for baptisms. As baptismal practice became more closely associated with the celebration of Easter, the ritual actions associated with baptism were reframed and reinterpreted around the themes of particular biblical texts. A service that places the reading of Exodus 12 alongside baptism suggests links between the two that might otherwise go unnoticed. In his examination of homilies from ancient Syria, church historian Karl Gerlach notes the growing preference for baptismal interpretations of this text.[15] Cyril of Jerusalem recognized in this typological approach a connection between Christ and the one being baptized. In reflecting on Cyril's instructions to the newly baptized and speaking of this association, liturgical theologian Dirk Lange notes: "When I enter the waters—whether as an adult or as a child—I enter into the fellowship of Christ's pain, of Christ's suffering and death."[16] This fellowship is linked with the call to attend to the suffering of the world. Resurrection occurs through our acts of mercy in the world around us. "We are raised up—our light 'shall rise'—we will know the resurrection when we are immersed in the fellowship of Christ's pain, immersed in the suffering of this world."[17]

Biblical reflection and communal experience in the early church coalesced around the central themes of baptism as initiation into a community of faith rooted in Jesus Christ's ministry, death, and resurrection. For these communities on the margins of society (which at times were forced to meet secretly and under great duress), a sense of solidarity with the suffering of Christ was no desire for martyrdom. Rather, they viewed their own struggles for faithfulness in welcoming and caring for strangers and the marginalized through the prism of the Christ narrative.

Leading by Example

The movement from renunciation to resurrection lies at the heart of the baptismal liturgy. This vision of baptismal life challenges congregations to turn from sin and to trust God by living into the hope of new life together. People want leaders whose lives provide a witness to this theology. This is not a call to perfectionism, but a call to speak of the honest struggles that we all face in living out the demands of the gospel. Recent psychological studies have indicated the rise of narcissism and self-importance in our culture. In its recent emphasis on entrepreneurial leadership, the church runs the risk of creating leaders whose own charisma becomes the central ingredient in congregational growth. Once again, the church is called to offer a countercultural model of leadership that values openness and transparency, one that welcomes the gifts of others and affirms the importance of seeking consensus. Effective congregational leaders embody the values of the renunciation in their lives. They turn away from our society's preoccupation with materialism and consumption to display in their own lives as disciples a sense of trust in Christ's grace and love.

For Amy, our baptismal candidate, these values were ultimately persuasive. While she continued to worry about her own ability to distance herself from her past, she began to see that renunciation was not dependent upon her own skill to forge a new path. These questions provided a way to express her trust in God's faithfulness and her willingness to live in a community whose members held one another accountable to the gospel's vision of God's reign. As she looked at her pastor, her mentors, and others around her in this community, she recognized in them a sense of hope about the possibility of release from the preoccupation with success, fame, and individual achievement. She had been welcomed by members of the community from the time she had slipped into the back pew of the church, and they had continued to support her through difficult transitions in her life. Through this body of Christ she heard, saw, felt, and encountered the gospel. Because of these experiences, she presented herself, doubts and all, to receive the sacrament of baptism.

MEDITATION 4

When the Spirit Moves

JOHN 7:37–39; ACTS 2:1–21

For seven days, people carried water into the temple. Each morning the rabbi took the large golden pitcher down to the fountain on the hillside below the temple and filled it to the top. Crowds gathered to watch as the priest lifted up the pitcher and carried it on his shoulder back into the temple. As he led the march up the hill, the choir led the people in singing the same song we sang here this morning:

With joy you shall draw water from the springs of endless life;
With joy you shall draw water from the living well of God.[1]

Over and over, the people sang out the words as they marched into the temple. This was the Feast of Tabernacles, a time to give thanks for God's providing in the past and a time to ask God's blessing on the crops in the coming year.

When they were all in the temple, the rabbi gathered the children in a circle around the altar. On the seventh day of the feast, they danced around the altar seven times. Slowly, the rabbi poured the water through a silver funnel, out onto the temple floor. The children giggled and laughed as the cold water trickled over their feet. Then the rabbi took the children aside and told them a story of how God gave water to save the people.

Once upon a time, we were wandering in the wilderness. Times were hard and there was nothing to drink. People were frightened and began to cry out to Moses. "Why did we come all the way

here if there is no water? We cannot live like this any longer." God
heard the cry of the people, and when Moses hit the rock with his
staff, water came rushing out.

In our Gospel reading today, Jesus joins in the annual festivities of
the Feast of Tabernacles. As he watches and listens to the stories of
the past, Jesus recognizes the present need of the people surrounding him. "Let anyone who is thirsty come to me, and let the one
who believes in me drink" (John 7:37–38). It is a shocking call to
those who have come simply to remember the past. Suddenly, the
town's festivities have a new sense of urgency to them. This is no
longer just a quaint reminder. It is a call to respond to our ongoing thirst. Not everyone is happy about this turn of events. John
tells us that some of the crowd want to have Jesus arrested for
disturbing the peace. The religious leaders in Jerusalem are getting
nervous about losing control of the ceremonies.

Jesus brings the rituals of the people to life. When liturgy connects with our present needs, then we can no longer sit quietly in
the pew and watch what is happening. Suddenly, we feel our own
thirst for answers that will last. Our dry throats call out for living
water. "Out of the believer's heart shall flow rivers of living water"
(John 7:38). The gift of this water comes not just miraculously
from above; this water breaks into our lives and flows out of us.
This water rises up within us so that we *may* serve one another.

That is precisely what we celebrate together here this morning
as we gather around this font to baptize Ray Ayers. Baptism is not
just water that the church provides to make for a nice ceremony.
Baptism is a declaration that God's living waters cover us and
burst up within us. For the past few weeks, Ray and I have been
meeting to talk about what baptism means. I am deeply impressed
by the way he has talked to me about what this water means to
him: baptism as belonging, as becoming part of a family, and as a
recognition of an ongoing change in his life.

This is not just a pleasant rite to sit back and enjoy. Baptism
calls us all to recognize our thirst for God's presence and to recon-
nect with the living water that flows in us and around us. It is this
water that can unite us and bring us together. For this water leads
us to the deep water within each of us. "Out of the believer's heart
shall flow rivers of living water."

PART III

Baptism

CHAPTER 5

Water

HE SAT QUIETLY ON A CHAIR behind a bowl of water that sat atop an overturned bucket, waiting for the Earth Day service to start. The chapel slowly began to fill with students, staff, and faculty. When we had all arrived, he started drumming on the water, slowly at first, but as the sounds of the piano provided texture, he picked up the pace. When his hands beat on the water in a percussive interlude, droplets jumped out of the bowl and onto the floor. Together, the sounds and sight of the water mesmerized us all. And then, as quickly as it had begun, it was over: the water gone from the bowl, the prelude over, the call to worship complete. The water had done its work.[1]

Water does not belong to the church. We use it, but it is not ours; it is an essential part of God's creation. Life depends on water. We drink it. We wash with it. We grow our food with it. We bathe in it. Growing awareness of the global ecological crisis is causing us to examine the ways we use water. Recent droughts and floods highlight the impact of having not enough water or too much of it at once. Current battles for water rights underscore the realization that access to clean water is a vital part of a sustainable future. We are learning that we can no longer afford to take clean water for granted. This awareness connects us with people of other times and places who were keenly aware of their daily reliance on water.

In the documentary *Water and Its Powers*, the filmmakers chronicle the significance of water in people's daily lives and ritual practices. Their survey of water's role throughout ancient and modern societies leads them to conclude: "Hence the widely accepted idea that water is the great Mother of the universe; the prime element at the origin of all things."[2] The use of water in our lives runs the gamut from the ordinary to the sacred. Water is a central part of the rituals of major religions. The poet Philip Larkin writes:

> *If I were called in*
> *To construct a religion*
> *I should make use of water.*[3]

People have used water in their religious rituals throughout time. Indigenous people prayed to the rain god to send water to sustain their crops and lives. Cleansing and purification rituals are a central part of most religious traditions. Hindus make a pilgrimage to the banks of the Ganges River, where they wash their bodies in the waters of the river, believing in the healing power of this sacred stream. Muslims use water in preparation for prayer. During the time of Jesus, proselytes to the Jewish religion were baptized. Many scholars have pointed to similar water rituals in mystery religions of the same era. Thus, it comes as no surprise that Christians would use water as a central element in worship. What is surprising is the lack of clear information about the history and interpretation of baptism in the early church.

Searching through Scripture

Christian baptismal practices clearly draw on the Gospel narratives of Jesus's baptism in the Jordan River by John the Baptist. Interpreters of this event immediately faced a difficult task, however. John's baptism was for the forgiveness of sin, a point that prompted Matthew to insert an explanation into the baptismal account. In Matthew, when Jesus stepped forward for baptism, John tried to prevent it, saying that there was no need for him to baptize Jesus. Matthew and other interpreters distanced themselves from the portrayal of Jesus as one who responds to a call to repentance. Instead, the emphasis was placed on Jesus as one who shows solidarity with sinners. Matthew's baptismal account was also portrayed as John's call to reform Jewish religious practices. John's preaching

was directed at the policies and practices of Pharisees and Saddu-
cees who misinterpreted the law. Baptism was an act of renewal
within Judaism to prepare for God's reign. John the Baptist was
drawing from accepted practices of the time. Reform movements
like Qumran included ritual practices with water for cleansing and
entrance into the community.[4] There is no single, clear interpretation for the development of Christian baptismal practices.

Further complicating the history of baptismal practice is the am-
bivalence in the Gospel of John about the role of baptism in Jesus's
own circle of disciples. We read of this tension in chapter 4. The
Pharisees have learned that "Jesus is making and baptizing more
disciples than John" (John 4:1). The narrator quickly inserts a word
of clarification: it was not actually Jesus but his disciples who were
baptizing. Regardless of who was baptizing (Jesus or his disciples),
we are left with questions about the meaning of this baptismal practice. Was this a continuation of John the Baptist's renewal movement, or was it the beginning of a different kind of movement?

What is certain about the early Christian practice of baptism is
that it quickly became an act that defined the community. In one
of the earliest reports in Acts, Peter's sermon at Pentecost echoes
the message of John the Baptist: repent and be baptized. This time,
though, the baptism is "in the name of Jesus Christ" (Acts 2:38).
In a relatively brief period, the earliest followers of Jesus adopted
baptism as an initiation rite for those desiring to become disciples
of Jesus Christ. The clarification that baptism was in the name
of Jesus is amplified in the story of Paul's visit to Ephesus, where
disciples had never heard of the Holy Spirit. When Paul inquired
about their baptism, they responded that they were baptized "into
John's baptism" (Acts. 19:3). Paul replied that John's baptism was
one of repentance, and the group of disciples was then "baptized
in the name of the Lord Jesus" (v. 5). This incident suggests that
an ongoing process of clarifying language in the baptismal formula
took place among early Christians. Relatively quickly, however, it
appears that the use of the trinitarian formula became customary.
The use of the Great Commission text in Matthew 28 provides
the primary support for this baptismal language. The risen Christ
instructed his disciples to go out, make other disciples, and baptize
them "in the name of the Father and of the Son and of the Holy

Spirit" (v. 19). (Still, the important point to note is that Matthew was offering encouragement and instructions to Jesus's disciples and not a required liturgical text.[5])

Scripture provides evidence of diverse baptismal practice and interpretations. From the various meanings of Jesus's baptism to the widely differing descriptions of baptismal practice in the early church, we can find a collage of images that depict ways communities adapted baptismal practices.

Local Contexts

Even the use of water in baptism went through significant transitions as the Christian movement expanded. The earliest baptisms were performed in rivers and other large bodies of water. By the second century, directions are given for the preferred mode of baptism.

> Now about baptism: this is how to baptize. Give public instruction on all these points, and then "baptize" in running water, "in the name of the Father and of the Son and of the Holy Spirit." If you do not have running water, baptize in some other. If you cannot in cold, then in warm. If you have neither, then pour water on the head three times "in the name of the Father, Son, and Holy Spirit."[6]

In this passage, we see the adoption of the trinitarian formula (from Matthew 28) as well as recognition of the need to adjust baptismal practices in settings that have limited access to water.

One of the most surprising developments of recent research in liturgical studies is the growing consensus around the diversity of worship practices in the early centuries of the church. While weekly Eucharist and baptismal initiation were core rituals, they were carried out in distinctly different ways in different communities. Eucharistic meals ran a wide gamut from full meals (1 Cor. 11) to a simple meal of bread and water. Some communities included milk and honey in the meal gathering; others used olive oil alongside the bread and wine. Liturgical scholar Paul Bradshaw notes: "There are also some signs that in certain communities other foodstuffs may have accompanied the bread and water (or wine) at the ritual meals and a thanksgiving said over them."[7] Finally, the Synod of Hippo in 393 C.E. passed a rule stipulating that only bread and wine mixed with water were allowed on the communion table.[8]

Similarly, baptismal practices developed distinct patterns. We have already surveyed a diverse selection of New Testament images, formulas, and patterns for baptism. Christian baptism was influenced by a wide variety of ritual practices from other religious traditions as well as from Roman bathing customs. After surveying the biblical images, liturgical scholar Bryan Spinks concludes:

> The New Testament is both the fulcrum from which emerges all theological reflection on baptism and all Christian baptismal rites, and the touchstone, or "norming norm" against which they may be tested. However, the books of the New Testament present neither a single doctrine of baptism, nor some archetypal liturgical rite.[9]

There is a growing recognition among scholars that as the Christian movement spread across the Roman Empire, baptismal practices took on distinctive features of local communities. The practices of anointing before and/or after bathing quickly became a customary part of baptism. Local communities likely followed regional cultural customs in their choices of when to anoint the individual and other bathing customs that became part of the baptismal liturgy. For example, some Christian communities adopted the use of incense, while others used ritual lamps and torches. Over time these ritual elements were given theological interpretations (e.g., oil is for sealing and preservation, or light is for illumination). Spinks concludes his analysis of the documents from the first three centuries: "We find different ritual patterns. . . . Thus the different ritual patterns found in the early Christian evidences mirror secular bathing customs."[10]

Growth and Uniformity

We have already seen how the rapid growth of Christianity in the fourth century dramatically altered the nature of baptismal preparation. This period of expansion also brought noteworthy change to baptismal practice itself. The shift from house churches to large buildings affected all areas of worship life. In some places, churches were constructed atop the sites of Roman baths to provide baptismal space. In other sites, baptismal pools were built in areas separate from the regular worship space.

Changes in baptismal theology also brought substantial change to baptismal practice. The emphasis on extended baptismal preparation with its call to change one's lifestyle prompted many Roman citizens to delay baptism. The emperor Constantine himself represented this shift. For two decades, he delayed receiving baptism. Only when he became ill late in his life did he make final baptismal preparations. Constantine's postponement of baptism "established a pattern of dithering and deathbed conversion (baptism called 'clinical' because it took place in bed [*kline*]) that would be common until infant baptism became normal practice."[11]

As the act of baptism increasingly focused on the cleansing of sins, inquirers worried about what would happen to them if they committed sins after their baptism. Preachers increasingly turned their attention to urging and pleading with listeners to follow through and receive baptism, and threatening that if they were not baptized, they would face the consequences of failing to receive the forgiveness found only in baptism.[12] The problem of delayed baptism was resolved in an unlikely manner. With an increasing preoccupation with the doctrine of original sin, Christian parents became concerned about the fate of their infants and children should they die before being baptized. While documents attest to the baptism of infants from at least the second century, adult baptism appears to have predominated. Augustine's theological emphasis on original sin underscored the need for infants to be baptized without delay. Alan Kreider comments:

Augustine initiated a "baptismal revolution" that unleashed pastoral and theological forces that fundamentally altered the primitive Christian pattern. Henceforth in the West it would become increasingly difficult not to baptize a newborn immediately; parents became fearful of the spiritual risks of deferring baptism until the paschal season. The ramifications of this transformation—ritual, theological, and pastoral—would profoundly shape the character of Christendom.[13]

As this new understanding of baptism took hold, church laws shifted to reflect these practices. Infants were required to be baptized within eight days of their birth. Cleansing from original sin received primary focus. The act of baptism became increasingly codified by the use of water with a required baptismal formula.[14]

Learning from the Past

This quick historical sketch points to significant shifts in baptismal practice during the early centuries of the church. From its beginning as a renewal rite in a river to its adoption as a spiritual cleansing for infants, the act of baptism shifted along with its theological interpretation. For the purposes of this study, the primary gleaning is recognition of the historical diversity of baptismal practices and the multivalent nature of the ritual act itself. As we have already seen, the New Testament itself provides a host of nuanced interpretations of baptism. The task for the church in our time is not to insist on one baptismal model and theological interpretation, but to learn to draw from the wealth of the biblical and historical resources to reinvigorate our own baptismal practice and theology.

The study of historical resources, the efforts of the ecumenical movement, and the work of the liturgical renewal movement have come together to bring significant change to baptismal practice. We will briefly examine four areas of baptismal practice that are undergoing significant change:

1. Baptism as a congregational act.
2. Design of architectural space for baptism.
3. Increased use of water.
4. Worship books and the recovery of baptismal imagery.

BAPTISM AS AN ACT OF THE COMMUNITY

Historical shifts in baptismal practice and theology reinforced the tendency to see baptism as a ritual that addressed the need of one individual—in many cases, an infant suffering from the plight of original sin. The requirement for infant baptism shortly after birth

shifted the practice of baptism away from being an act of the congregation. Increasingly, baptism became a private event performed
by priests and on some occasions by midwives.[15] In her brilliant
study of baptismal practice in Geneva at the time of the Reformation, Karen Spierling documents the difficult transition led by John
Calvin and other Reformers to reclaim the act of baptism within
the context of the congregation's worship life.

> The reformers transformed the baptismal ceremony from an of-
> ten-private to an always-public ritual, forcing it out of the realm
> of families and midwives and into the arena of church and city au-
> thority. . . . Thus, Reformed baptism was, eventually, clearly estab-
> lished as a public ceremony with faithful Christian participants.[16]

While the reclamation of baptism as a congregational act in the
context of worship has become normative throughout the ecumenical church, tensions remain. Recently, a pastor from an affluent
congregation told me of a request he had received from a promi-
nent family in his congregation. "Pastor, we have set the date and
time for our son's baptism for a week from Saturday. We have
sent out invitations and hired a caterer. We just need you to show
up and do your part!" Here, baptism as a family event and social
occasion provided the primary lens. The pastor was left with the
task of managing a lengthy conversation about the place and significance of baptism.

As we have seen, the recovery of a vibrant baptismal theology
is predicated on the congregation's role in providing space, welcome, mentors, and training to nurture and support individuals as
they move toward baptism. The act of baptism becomes a mutual
dialogue between an individual and a congregation. Together, the
congregation celebrates the individual's response to God's grace as
a fellow disciple of Jesus Christ. The landmark ecumenical docu-
ment *Baptism, Eucharist and Ministry* recognizes the significance
of baptism occurring within the context of worship:

> Since baptism is intimately connected with the corporate life and
> worship of the Church, it should normally be administered during
> public worship, so that the members of the congregation may be

reminded of their own baptism and may welcome into their fellowship those who are baptized and whom they are committed to
nurture in the Christian faith.[17]

Recovering the primary role of the congregation as those who welcome, nurture, and support those who seek baptism is a primary
goal of worship renewal.

MAKING SPACE FOR BAPTISM

The new cathedral in Managua, Nicaragua, offers an architectural
vision of baptismal space. One enters the front corner of the vast
sanctuary and discovers a rock with a rough-hewn opening to hold
water. The dark room is illuminated solely by a skylight directly
above the baptismal rock, literally a hole in the ceiling through
which the sun shines on the baptismal area. One of the rough concrete walls is painted with a large mural presenting baptism as a
dreamlike sequence. On the left side of the wall, John the Baptist
stands knee-deep in a large stream of water with his right hand
stretched out, pointing off in the distance to Jesus, who is enter-
ing the water. On the right side of the mural, a larger portrait
of the risen Christ, still partially submerged in the water, depicts
him with wounded hand upraised and blessing all who enter the
space. A disciple kneels in adoration at his side, and Christ's hand
is placed on the head of the disciple to bestow a blessing. In the
middle of the mural, a naked adult in a fetal position with arms
crossed in the sign of a cross is pushed completely beneath the water by one who stands in the stream to perform the baptism, while
the shimmering gown of the risen Christ floats in waves through
the rippling water and extends toward the one being baptized as
another form of blessing.

This remarkable work of art situates each baptism that takes
place here within the movement of the biblical narrative. The architecture itself provides a theological commentary on the act of
baptism. Standing near a rock from which the water comes, il-
lumined by the light from above (shining through a hole in the
roof), dwarfed by a mural of Christ's baptism and resurrection,
the baptismal candidate is drawn into the gospel narratives. She

becomes a recipient of the water that springs from the rock in the
Exodus narrative. The heavens are opened above her, and she is
declared a beloved child of God. Her body assumes the place in the
mural of the one submerged beneath the Jordan River alongside
Jesus who comes to be baptized and the risen Christ who rises out
of the water.

Clearly, not all church architecture provides such a dramatic
setting. Nevertheless, congregations experiencing worship renewal
are giving increased attention to baptismal space. Several years ago
when I was being interviewed by a committee seeking to call a new
pastor, the committee chair took me to see the church's sanctuary.
I looked around the beautiful Spanish-style building and admired
the stunning stained-glass windows. The sanctuary was decorated
lavishly for the coming Christmas celebration. The baptismal font
was nowhere in sight. Finally, I asked where the font was. "Oh, we
keep our baptismal bowl locked up in the silver closet and bring
it out whenever we need it." When I accepted the call to serve as
pastor in the congregation, the bowl came out of the closet and became part of our gathering space. Slowly but surely, congregations
are reclaiming the significance of baptismal space. Pulpit, table,
and font together provide the architectural vocabulary that points
to the center of our faith. Since Vatican II, many Roman Catholic congregations have made significant architectural renovations
in their sanctuaries. Reclaiming the model of the catechumenate
(Rite of Christian Initiation of Adults) led many Roman Catholic
parishes to examine their baptismal space, and many congregations have added pools that allow for baptisms by immersion.

Increasingly, liturgical leaders are emphasizing the importance
of baptismal space as central to the recovery of a robust baptismal
theology. Liturgical historians have carefully documented the drastic reduction in baptismal space from the baptismal pools of early
churches to small, covered containers. Other changes in baptismal
place have taken place. During the Middle Ages, baptismal water
was associated with magical powers, and holy water was stolen
for its curative powers as well as for its alleged property of increasing fertility rates in livestock. As a result, lids (sometimes with
locks) were added to the baptismal fonts of many churches. When
baptismal space is diminished in size, removed from the sanctuary,

or hidden behind curtains, then the central, ongoing claims of baptism are removed from our regular worship experiences.

ADDING WATER

Each semester, I show my students a clip of the 1992 art movie *Tango Lessons*. It is a beautiful film about two Jewish characters—Sally, a woman who directs movies, and Pablo, a famous tango dancer. She decides to take lessons from him to learn the tango. The dance lessons chronicle the story of their budding romance, which is finally interrupted by a difficult argument. Sally ends up at St. Sulpice, in Paris, where she stands inside the church gazing at a picture of Jacob wrestling with the angel. She walks out of the church, calls Pablo, and asks him to meet her at the church. There beneath the picture they pose their bodies in a mirror image of Jacob's encounter with God (which led to his wounded hip). Then she leads him to the fountain outside the church and slowly sprinkles water on his forehead. He responds by sprinkling water on her forehead. Next, she presses his face into the water of the fountain. Suddenly, he is completely submerged, swimming in the depths of the water. The scene switches to the couple looking out the window of a cab through the pouring rain. "Do you feel like you have come home again?" she asks him. Together, they climb out into the rain and dance their way down the street before slowly embracing.

I always ask my students to reflect on what they see in this film clip. Sometimes they seem reluctant to say much. On one occasion, a woman raised her hand, hesitated for a minute, and finally blurted out, "It seemed kind of sensuous." That is precisely the point. Baptism is an embodied act. We make significant theological claims at baptism. We speak of rebirth, of moving from death to new life, of being named as a beloved child of God. These claims demand actions that demonstrate the significance of these events in our lives. Water is the primary component of baptism. Thus, it is important that ample amounts of water be used in the act of baptism to accompany the claims we make. Christian faith is a way of life shared together. Our rituals mark this journey. Baptism as the initiation rite deserves to be fully embodied and celebrated.

As a parish pastor, I regularly met with parents of infants and baptismal candidates. Part of the preparation was to talk about the baptismal service itself. Together we would go through the liturgy and look at the questions they would be asked. I also was careful to speak of the central role of water and how those being baptized would get wet during the service. People were sometimes surprised to hear this and expressed concern about protecting their clothes or not having their hair messed up. If concern for how one will look takes primary importance, then I think that it is fair to ask if the individual is ready to live out a call to discipleship that is countercultural to much of today's society. Water has been used for cleansing and purification rituals from ancient times, and Christians share this practice with people of widely different faith traditions. Water's role as a cleansing agent reinforces the importance of using ample amounts of water, whether baptism is performed by sprinkling, pouring, or immersion. However, baptismal imagery is not limited to notions of purity (and indeed, the Gospels depict Jesus's ongoing critique of some religious leaders' obsession with Jewish purity codes). An abundant use of water in baptism also shows connections to other theological themes associated with baptism. Clearly, the practice of immersion best embodies Paul's baptismal commentary in Romans: "Do you not know that all of us who have been baptized into Christ Jesus were baptized into his death? Therefore we have been buried with him by baptism into death, so that, just as Christ was raised from the dead by the glory of the Father, so we too might walk in newness of life" (Rom. 6:3–4).

BAPTISMAL IMAGERY IN LITURGICAL RESOURCES

The recovery of a fuller baptismal liturgy has been aided by the publication of denominational worship books, which have steadily provided a richer liturgical rite. The development of these resources continues to push congregations toward the ecumenical vision of recognizing the validity of baptism among all Christians. Learning from one another as well as from the past provides an opportunity for shared baptismal practice. Gordon Lathrop, a leading liturgical scholar, notes the growing agreement on a shared shape (*ordo*) of baptismal preparation and practice. Lathrop summarizes the liturgical pattern for baptism developed at a Faith and Order Consultation in Ditchingham, England:

Formation in faith
Water-washing
Participation in the life of the community.[18]

Recent worship books and resources reinforce the movement toward a shared understanding and practice of baptism with a richer baptismal liturgy. Presbyterian congregations are now reclaiming the practice of adult baptisms. Before the reunion of the northern and southern denominations in 1983, the Directory for Worship in the (southern) Presbyterian Church (U.S.) provided minimal instructions for baptizing only infants. In the context of a "Christian culture," the practice of adult baptism received little consideration. New liturgical resources continue to offer broader services and commentary on baptismal practice.[19]

In addition to including new baptismal rites, recent worship resources draw more widely on baptismal imagery. In its service of Morning Prayer, *Evangelical Lutheran Worship*, produced by the Evangelical Lutheran Church in America, includes a Thanksgiving for Baptism consisting of a baptismal hymn, the pouring of water, a prayer replete with baptismal imagery, the option of baptismal remembrance by sprinkling the congregation with water, a closing prayer with baptismal language, and the passing of the peace.[20] New worship resources increasingly are adopting baptismal imagery to use throughout all of the church's services. In chapter 7, we will examine this movement more closely as we reflect on the significance of baptism as a lifelong journey.

Moving Forward

The recovery of a fuller baptismal practice remains a work in progress in many congregations. A recent graduate returned to our Presbyterian seminary campus and reported that at the first baptism where he presided, he was accused of being Baptist because he "used too much water." Resistance remains in places where people report that worship has never been done this way before.

Despite this reluctance, many people (both inside and outside the church) thirst for worship that is fully embodied, that speaks to body, mind, and soul, and that is rich in symbols, gestures, and rituals. Congregational leaders working at worship renewal are discovering the power of services that embody the theological claims of baptism to take root in our lives. Baptism, where water is visibly and audibly central to the action, breaks open the dry, overly cognitive explanations that are sometimes offered. Water to wade in, water to pour, water to lift up, water that we see and hear prompts our imaginations to envision a new way of life.

At a Sunday morning service in early January, a family of four sat in a front row of the sanctuary surrounded by family and friends. On this day, mother, father, and the two children would all be baptized. It was a joyous occasion, a sign of new life not only for this family, but for all of us who gathered there. The baptismal liturgy was expansive, and water was used generously. After presiding at the service, I stood near the door of the church. Many were thrilled by the richness of the service, but I also heard one person question whether it was appropriate for people "to get that wet in church." This struggle to make the church less concerned about appearances and more involved in God's transformation of our lives and our world is what baptism is ultimately about. Because of this, our actions, our words, and our gestures point to the disruptive possibility that baptism displays for us. With water that comes from creation, we act in faith as a way of living into the hope of God's promises for our lives and for our world.

MEDITATION 5

Keeping the
Right Wardrobe

MARK 9:2–9

I don't need to tell you that the church faces intense pressures to change. We face this pressure every day of the week. Today I want to talk with you about a way to negotiate the winds of change. Our Gospel reading offers a surprising wardrobe tip on where to find that dazzling outfit.

Embedded in this story of Jesus's visit to a mountaintop with some of his disciples is a set of snapshots from an earlier story of Jesus's baptism in the Jordan River by John the Baptist. It is a kind of cinematic flashback to the beginning of Mark's Gospel. Mark starts not with a nativity scene or Christmas Eve story, but with Jesus's baptism. For Mark, Jesus is born here in the Jordan River. Out of this seminal experience, the teaching, healing, and feeding ministry begins.

The scene of Jesus's baptism opens with John the Baptist out in the wilderness. John is famous for his fashion faux pas—that tacky (and out-of-date) attire of camel's hair and a leather belt. This retro outfit is a mistaken tribute to his hero, the prophet Elijah. John the Baptist is a hardworking preacher pressing for change. He is a populist calling for renewal, pleading his case out in the wilderness, far from the center of religious and political power in Jerusalem. The wilderness gathering is part religious revival and part circus spectacle, and evidently everyone wants to participate. Jesus joins the crowd that gathers in the wilderness, and he is baptized in the Jordan River—the same river where Elijah and Elisha met to pass the prophetic mantle; the same Jordan River that Moses looked across to see the Promised Land; the river the children of Israel had crossed on their journey of discipleship.

While the Old Testament stories of the Jordan River picture the water opening up, at Jesus's baptism the water closes over him while the sky appears to have ripped open, and the Spirit descends. Here in the waters of baptism, Jesus receives a divine blessing. Here in the waters of baptism, Jesus's ministry begins. After his baptism, Jesus heads out on the road, preaching the news of God's reign. As conflict begins to escalate between Jesus and the religious leaders in Jerusalem, Jesus goes off on a spiritual retreat with James and Peter and John. In today's reading, they escape the crowds and head high up the mountain to regroup. It is there on the mountain that Mark describes a mystical scene of transfiguration.

Here, on the mountaintop, we get a fashion show that is simply divine. Jesus appears before the disciples in a dazzling white outfit. It would be easy to overlook the meaning of Jesus's choice of attire, to dismiss it as a laser-show gimmick on a first-century runway, but Mark will not let us rush past this fashion statement. In case we miss the point of the outfit, Mark provides us other clues about its meaning. Elijah and Moses show up as the judges of this fashion show. A cloud overshadows the entire scene—always a sign of God's presence—and from the cloud comes the same voice from Jesus's baptism with a strikingly similar message. "This is my Son, the Beloved. Listen to him!"

In Mark's Gospel, this transfiguration tale occurs in the exact middle of the gospel. We have seen the journey from baptism to the mountain. Beginning with today's transfiguration experience, Jesus travels back down the mountain to the cross in Jerusalem. Throughout this long journey, Jesus lives out his baptismal experience.

There will be challenging days, as conflicts and a confrontation with the religious and political authorities lie ahead. In the midst of all this turmoil, this dazzling white cloth—this sign of baptismal identity as a child of God that is wrapped around Jesus like swaddling clothes—will surround him.

Lately I have been reading quite a bit about baptism in the good old days. By "good old days," I mean way back seventeen hundred or eighteen hundred years ago when Christianity was still a young religion. Back then, if you showed an interest in Christianity, you underwent a kind of preliminary examination called a "scrutiny." The test consisted of one question: Were you willing to help out those who were in need? If you were, then you went through a time of preparation for baptism, which in some places lasted for a couple of years. During this time, the primary purpose of the training was to work on caring for your neighbors—not just the people around you whom you liked, but the widows, orphans, prisoners, and strangers from foreign countries. These folks who otherwise were neglected were made the focus of attention. In fact, Christians became known as the people who took food and clothes to those who were usually ignored. Baptismal preparation involved spending time and energy caring for the forgotten. When you had made enough progress on this journey, you were brought before the congregation, and one of the regulars in the congregation stood beside you and testified on your behalf. "I have been watching George, and I have noticed that he spends time caring for the sick and poor, and I see signs of growth in his life." Once you had made it that far, then there was a crash course during Lent to prepare you for the big event of your baptism at Easter. You learned the Lord's Prayer and the Apostles' Creed. Then, at the vigil on the eve of Easter, those who were going to be baptized gathered and were taken to the water, where they were baptized in the name of the Father, and the Son, and the Holy Spirit. When they came up out of the pool of water, they were wrapped in new white clothes—their baptismal gowns. Afterward, everyone gathered around a table to share a meal, a celebration, a feast of bread and wine, and sometimes of milk and honey. This bread and this cup, which we still share today, became the weekly event where baptized Christians came together—to renew our baptismal vows, to encourage one another, and to continue to go out to feed and clothe our neighbors.

Brothers and sisters in Christ, I do not know all the challenges you face, but ministry always comes with its own sets of opportunities and demands. Surely, your neighborhood includes those who are poor, forgotten, and neglected. Reaching out is rewarding and sometimes difficult work. It can be easy to get so caught up in the significant moments we share inside these walls that we forget our

primary mission to live as disciples of Jesus Christ who respond
to the needs of those around us. Today's Gospel reading points us
clearly back in this direction, however. On the mountaintop with
Jesus, Peter becomes so caught up in the moment that he suggests
that they should stay. But then the divine cloud envelops Jesus and
the disciples, and they remember their baptisms and head down
the mountain to continue their ministry.

Friends, our baptismal clothes prepare us for the work that
God is calling us to do. Our common experiences at this font and
around this table prepare us and strengthen us for the days ahead.
Today may the Spirit wrap us and clothe us in the words of this
table prayer:

> *Teach us to befriend the lost,*
> *To serve the poor,*
> *To reconcile our enemies,*
> *And to love our neighbors.*[1]

As we go out from this place, my eyes will be looking at the dazzling white gowns that each of you is wearing. To God be the
glory. Amen.

PART IV

Baptismal Reflections

CHAPTER 6

Gifts

MANY YEARS AGO, AS A young pastor, I led a discussion at a meeting about the importance of identifying the gifts we bring to our communities. One by one, we participants went around the room and spoke about the gifts we recognized in our own lives. At the time, I was particularly surprised by Pam's observation as she succinctly summed up her sense of giftedness: "I smile at people." For a moment, it struck me as somewhat trivial, something any and all of us do from time to time. But as I pondered it more deeply, I was impressed by her clarity. She possessed a dazzling smile and exuded warmth, traits that were central to the hospitality she provided at church as well as at her family's restaurant down the street.

Throughout this book, we have been exploring baptism as an act that is not simply an end in itself. Most of our attention has focused on preparation for baptism and a life of discipleship. In this chapter, we turn our attention to the church's responsibility in helping the baptized discover their gifts and identify places to exercise these gifts. In the *Book of Common Worship*, the following prayer immediately follows the baptism itself and is accompanied by the laying on of hands:

O Lord, uphold N. by your Holy Spirit.
Give him/her the spirit of wisdom and understanding,
The spirit of counsel and might,
The spirit of knowledge and the fear of the Lord,
The spirit of joy in your presence,
Both now and forever. Amen.[1]

The significance of this prayer of blessing is related to the theological belief that baptism by water is accompanied by God's gift of the Holy Spirit. Most Christian churches believe that these are simultaneous acts. The prayer of thanksgiving before the baptism invokes the Spirit's presence over the water and asks that the Spirit be poured out on the one who will be baptized. The water baptism itself is bracketed by these prayers as a way to show the interrelationship of water and Spirit. Christian baptism invokes the Spirit's presence as a distinctive way that connects the ceremonial use of water in the context of worship with the gift of new identity as a beloved child of God.

The fusion of water and the Spirit is found in the Gospel story of Jesus's baptism. John baptizes with water but declares that the One who is to come will baptize with the Spirit. Baptismal practice in the early church connected these images. Luke portrays the connection in the baptismal narrative in Acts 19. The apostle Paul meets a group of disciples in Ephesus and inquires whether they have received the Holy Spirit. They respond that they have not even heard of the Holy Spirit. Paul then diagnoses the problem as one of baptismal malfunction: the disciples have received John's baptism of repentance, but they have not been baptized in the name of Jesus and received the Holy Spirit. After they are baptized in the name of the Lord Jesus, Paul lays hands on them and they receive the gift of the Holy Spirit (Acts 19:1–6). The gift of the Spirit in Christian baptism is connected to the discovery of particular gifts for service. This chapter examines gifts within the context of the community of faith as well as gifts that individuals have to offer in their ministry in the world.

Family as Gift

Because baptism is a ritual of new birth, in baptism the person receives a new family. From the beginning of the church, Christians offered a startling new claim in a culture that was oriented around family clans. In his study of Pauline literature, New Testament scholar Scott Bartchy emphasizes the importance of siblings in the ancient Mediterranean world. Brothers and sisters provided the closest, most loyal bonds in the ancient world. Baptism dramatically redefines one's most profound relationships. Bartchy explains, "Paul's strategy in this regard was to exhort these new surrogate siblings in faith to treat each other as they had been socialized to treat their blood kin, but more so—specifically to *seek to outdo each other in showing honor to each other.*"[2]

Baptism offers us the gift of a new family, and the water family takes precedence over blood ties. Kinship is established through baptism. As beloved children of God, we are brothers and sisters in Christ. This family of faith promises to nurture us, so that together we may grow in faith. In this new family of faith, born of water and Spirit, Christians were urged to recognize the gifts that each one brought to form what Bartchy describes as "a well functioning family in the kinship sense, in which each family member used his or her strengths, whatever they were, first of all to enrich the quality of life in the family rather than for themselves as individuals."[3]

Today the image of congregation as family can lead to sentimental expectations that everyone in church will get along. In the Gospels the depiction of family was not one designed for Hallmark cards. This new family was identified as those who gathered to do God's will. Early in Mark's Gospel, Jesus presents this new family portrait when he is told that his mother and brothers and sisters are outside waiting for him. Jesus responds by pointing to those around him: "Here are my mother and my brothers! Whoever does the will of God is my brother and sister and mother" (Mark 3:34–35). As the disciples struggle to figure out these new relationships, they express concern about what they have given up to follow Jesus. Peter confronts Jesus: "Look, we have left our homes and followed you." Jesus replies, "There is no one who has left house or wife or brothers or parents or children, for the sake of the kingdom of God, who will not get back very much more in this age, and in the age to come eternal life" (Luke 18:28–30).

The gift of these new brothers and sisters requires a willingness to leave old family systems behind in pursuit of the gospel. In Luke, Jesus dismisses the claims of those who say they must first bury their father or say farewell to those at home before following him (Luke 9:57ff). Discipleship creates a new community of brothers and sisters. The significance of this radical reorganization of family ties is demonstrated in congregations where Christianity is a minority religion and joining the church comes with great risk. For example, in India members of the Dalit caste lose basic government privileges when they are baptized as Christians. Because Christianity is viewed as a foreign religion, its members are not eligible for the same benefits as Hindu, Sikh, or Buddhist Dalits. The government of India refuses to include Christian Dalits in the official list of castes, thus denying them the basic benefits guaranteed by the constitution.[4] A decision to become Christian places individuals at a new level of vulnerability and uncertainty.

In certain Islamic countries, a decision to convert to Christianity carries with it the threat of being disowned. In Egypt, baptism is often done secretly because of concerns over a Muslim backlash.[5] Religious historian Phillip Jenkins underscores the plight of crypto-Christians, Christians who hide their belief out of fear or reprisal from government, neighbors, or family.[6] In these situations, Christians find themselves challenged by systems that marginalize their communities. In these dire conditions, congregations practice care for one another as brothers and sisters in Christ.

I have not endured the negative consequences that Christians in some cultures face, but I have been embraced by a community that received me as family, and have experienced the positive effects of that welcome. When I was a graduate student in Germany, our family worshiped at the English Church in Heidelberg, a small, English-language, ecumenical congregation. Professionals and students intermingled. Friendships formed, and we welcomed one another into our homes and our lives. We celebrated holidays together. The level of care for one another was extraordinary. The congregation functioned as an extended family for those of us who were far from home. In all of these situations, those who are baptized recognize the gift of family that comes to those who belong to Christ.

Covenant as Gift

Church as family is closely connected to the image of the covenant community. The language is woven into the prayer of anointing following the baptism as well as in the words of welcome:

N., child of the covenant,
You have been sealed by the Holy Spirit in baptism,
And marked as Christ's own forever.
N. has been received into the one holy, catholic, and apostolic
    church through baptism.
God has made him/her a member of the household of God
To share with us in the priesthood of Christ.[7]

The one baptized is identified as God's child (no matter his or her age) who belongs to this covenant community.

The emphasis on covenant is of particular theological significance in some denominations. Reformed congregations have attached heightened importance to covenant as a central theological theme in baptism. In the Reformation era, John Calvin's dramatic revision of the baptismal rite grew out of the centrality of covenant in his theology. Calvin recast the baptismal service with an emphasis on salvation as dependent on God's grace and election. For Calvin, salvation was no longer considered a result of baptism. Baptism marked one's inclusion in a covenant community that lived together in thanksgiving. The practical implications of this shift were dramatic. Calvin outlawed private baptism. Baptisms once again took place during worship services. The promises made by the parents and the community stressed a relationship of trust and support in which the community pledged to teach and model faith to those who received baptism. For Calvin, according to Spierling:

> Baptism was a visible sign and seal of a person's entrance into
> the community of the faithful, asserting that the rite of baptism
> was not necessary for salvation, *and* still defending, like Luther,
> the place of baptism as a sacrament in which God is present and
> God's grace works in the participants.[8]

The act of baptism provides a witness to God's faithfulness in the covenant extended to us. The congregation as a whole serves as a primary participant in this new covenant as members renew their baptismal vows and pledge to teach and support the ones who are being baptized. This theological approach recognizes baptism as the act that seals the covenant that God extends to us.[9]

Anointing as Gift

The practice of anointing with oil drew upon common bathing practices of the time, which varied across the Greco-Roman empire. In some cultures, people were typically anointed before the water bath, while in other places anointing took place after the washing. As a result, Christian communities adopted diverse patterns, some anointing before the baptism; some, after; or others, both. The use of oil was believed to provide "a wide range of benefits—protective, preventive, mollifying, and cosmetic."[10] Over time, Christians provided theological interpretations of the practices they brought to their worship assemblies. By the second century, oil for anointing became a central part of the baptismal celebration.[11] In early third-century descriptions of baptismal practices, we find depictions of anointing as well as theological interpretations of the action. While anointing the whole body with oil was normative, the pouring of oil on the head was associated with the practice of anointing priests and kings in ancient Israel. In some places, the act of anointing on the head became associated with the words, "Thou art my Son, this day I have begotten you."[12] Thus, the anointing comes to refer specifically to Christ. By associating the act of anointing (and its historical significance in priestly and kingly preparation) with the narrative of Jesus's baptism, the early church combines theological emphases on coronation and new birth.[13]

In addition to connecting the cultural practice of anointing with scriptural texts, Christians could draw on layers of meaning from the popular culture as well. As Spinks explains, "While interpreting the anointing as messianic is distinctly Christian, the idea of anointing for protection and healing which we also find, simply spiritualized a commonly accepted secular understanding of the use of oil in bathing."[14] The practice of anointing carried multiple meanings for its participants.

In some congregations, specific kinds of oil were used for different parts of the service. Common oil (usually olive oil) was used to mark the inquirers who were preparing for baptism. This practice became associated with exorcism as the baptismal candidates renounced Satan and the powers of evil. A prayer of blessing on those who were about to be baptized accompanied the anointing: "Grant them your wisdom to understand the gospel more deeply and your strength to accept the challenge of Christian life. Enable them to rejoice in the baptism and to partake of a new life in the church as true children of your family."[15] The use of perfumed oil that was specially prepared and blessed (known as chrism) for anointing after the baptism became associated with gladness and thanksgiving. In the Roman Catholic baptismal rite, such anointing is accompanied by these words: "He now anoints you with the chrism of salvation. As Christ was anointed Priest, Prophet, and King, so may you live always as members of his body, sharing everlasting life."[16]

The extravagance of these actions led some to question their appropriateness as part of the service. John Calvin spoke out strongly against the use of oil, salt, and other elements associated with the baptismal service of his day.[17] His concern centered on the ways that other aspects of the service overshadowed the central role of water in baptism.[18] Many Protestant congregations now include anointing as part of the service,[19] however, and the reclamation of the ancient practice of anointing has become increasingly connected with the prayer for the Spirit's sealing of the baptism. Associations between the act of anointing and the language of the Spirit's work in the life of the baptized are woven together in the baptismal liturgy.

Baptism as Gift

It is important not to overlook the way that baptism is a gift in itself. Each year, I teach a seminary class on the sacraments. The class on baptism includes time for us to meet weekly in the chapel and practice the baptismal rite. Near the end of the semester, each student leads a brief service for the class that includes a short sermon and the complete baptismal service. On one occasion, Hyoung-Seop Shin, a graduate student from South Korea, brought a teenage boy with him from the congregation where he regularly worships. Following the sermon, he invited the boy to join him at the font. The baptismal prayer was beautifully recited (by memory!); water was generously poured over the young boy's head. Then, we watched as Hyoung-Seop took a small pitcher of oil and poured it on the boy's head. He gently rubbed the oil into the boy's hair as he prayed, "Child of the covenant, you have been sealed by the Holy Spirit in baptism, and marked as Christ's own forever. Amen."[20] When he finished, the class sat in stunned silence. We were so moved by the power of the service, the beauty of the presiding, and the extravagance of the gestures that we did not want the service to end. Finally, one of the students blurted out, "That was so incredible that I didn't know whether to applaud or cry when it was over."

In baptism, we celebrate that God names us as beloved children, welcomes us into the family of the church, and blesses us with gifts for ministry and service. Our celebration of these life-changing claims should be grand enough to carry the theological claims made. The rich, symbolic world of baptism provides us with multiple images. We need not restrict ourselves to a particular approach or meaning of baptism. Instead, as we have seen, Scripture offers a variety of perspectives, and Christians have developed a wide range of baptismal interpretations.

An example of the broad connections Christians historically have made with baptism is seen in the growing tendency of the early church to hold baptisms on Easter. The first followers of Jesus connected the Passover meal with their memories of Jesus's arrest, crucifixion, and resurrection. The early celebrations of Easter united cross and resurrection as one event that was remembered around a meal. The Passover tradition centered on a retelling of Exodus 12, the story of the Hebrew people crossing the Red Sea and leaving slavery behind in Egypt. The powerful imagery of this water story prompted listeners to develop associations between the Exodus 12 reading and their own baptismal practices. The ritual actions of baptism reframe and reinterpret biblical texts. A service that places the reading of Exodus 12 alongside baptism suggests links between the two that might otherwise go unnoticed. Homilies from ancient Syria showed a preference for developing baptismal typology in spite of attempts to develop eucharistic themes.[21] By the end of the second century, Tertullian recommended Easter as the preferred time for baptisms. Over time, the increasing frequency of baptism as part of the celebration of Easter prompted church leaders to use Lent as a time of intense preparation for those who were presented as baptismal candidates. In some parts of the church where catechumens prepared for two to three years, the length of the time leading up to their baptisms brought a heightened sense of anticipation.[22] The fifty days between Easter and Pentecost became a time for those who were baptized during the Easter service to reflect on their baptismal experience. Baptism became an interpretive lens that prompted Christians to hear biblical texts and shape their practices in a different way.

Gifts for Ministry

Christian communities emphasized a period of preparation and a time for reflection on baptism because of its central place as a rite of passage into the church. Designating a time for reflection on baptism is connected with an understanding of baptism as the occasion when Christians receive gifts for service. In this sense, rather than viewing baptism as a destination, we realize that baptism marks the beginning of a time of discernment when we discover gifts for ministry in the world. Earlier we explored the importance of mentors in preparing inquirers considering baptism. In a similar way, mentors can serve a crucial role in supporting those recently baptized by helping them find places of service in the congregation.

Congregations can help members discover their gifts for service by emphasizing the spiritual gifts given at baptism and providing occasions for these gifts to be named and exercised. While this practice may take different forms in various congregations, leaders should create opportunities to support individuals as they discover and exercise their gifts. In one congregation, for a time, our service started with a young person reading Galatians 5:22: "The fruit of the Spirit is love, joy, peace, patience, kindness, generosity, faithfulness, gentleness, and self-control." Each week, we emphasized one of these gifts. As the congregation sang together about the gifts of the Spirit, a young person took a framed picture of a member of our congregation who modeled this gift and hung the picture on a "tree of life" we constructed out of madrona limbs in a corner of the sanctuary. The power of this approach was that it helped connect images of the gifts of the Spirit with people in our congregation. The gifts of the Spirit were no longer abstract lists. We knew what these gifts looked like in the lives of members of our congregation.

Leaders can facilitate this discovery by helping the community recognize gifts and express thanksgiving for those who model them. Practices like these provide implicit role models for those new to the community. More formal mentoring opportunities can be developed to help new Christians grow in faith. Larger congregations may choose to hold post-baptismal classes to match newcomers with mentors, to help newcomers discern the gifts that they bring to the community, and to provide ministry opportunities for them to develop their gifts. Smaller congregations as a whole may be able to take on these tasks but will need to focus on nurturing newcomers and helping them grow into the life of the community.

Another possibility is to build on the role of sponsors throughout the baptismal journey. In one congregation, the community gathers for its regular worship service on Pentecost. After the sermon, the pastor invites those who were baptized at one of the Easter services and their congregational mentors/sponsors to join her by the baptismal font. She slowly pours a pitcher of water into the font and reads from Scripture: "You are a chosen race, a royal priesthood, a holy nation, God's own people, in order that you may proclaim the mighty acts of the One who called you out of darkness into God's marvelous light" (1 Pet. 2:9 NRSV, alt.).[23] The pastor then invites the sponsors to offer a brief testimony about the gifts these newcomers are bringing into the life of the congregation. Following the testimony, the pastor offers a brief prayer of thanksgiving about ways in which the Spirit is bringing new life to the congregation through the gifts and ministry offered by these newcomers.

A word of caution is appropriate at this point: institutions can become preoccupied with maintaining their own structures. While newcomers may well bring gifts they can use to serve within the

congregation, the purpose of the church is not primarily self-pres-
ervation. Rather it provides a place of welcome, hope, and good
news. Luke's Gospel summarizes Jesus's message as he begins his
public ministry by visiting his home synagogue in Nazareth. There
Jesus reads from the prophet Isaiah:

> *The Spirit of the Lord is upon me,*
> *because he has anointed me*
> > *to bring good news to the poor.*
> *He has sent me to proclaim release to the captives*
> > *and recovery of sight to the blind,*
> > *to let the oppressed go free,*
> *to proclaim the year of the Lord's favor.*
>
> —LUKE 4:18–19

The church as the body of Christ in the world lives out this call
by caring for the poor, the marginalized, the forgotten, and the
neglected. Just as baptismal preparation focuses on caring for our
neighbors and the world around us, so too the church's primary
responsibility is to welcome the stranger, feed the hungry, provide
for the thirsty, clothe the naked, and visit the sick and imprisoned (Matt. 25:31ff). Christians perform these tasks to discover
and encounter Christ, who is present with the marginalized and
neglected.[24]

Baptism also serves as the primary basis from which the church
recognizes the gifts for ordained ministry in the church. Newer
denominational worship resources increasingly show this integral
connection in their liturgies. For example, the ordination rites for
deacons, elders, and ministers for Presbyterians all begin with
scriptural references and baptismal imagery, such as this passage:
"As many of you as were baptized into Christ have clothed yourselves with Christ" (Gal. 3:27). This is followed by the presentation of those who will be ordained: "In baptism, N. and N. were
clothed with Christ and are now called by God through the voice
of the church to enter into ministries of service and governance,
announcing in word and deed the good news of Jesus Christ."[25]
The service also includes a reaffirmation of the baptismal covenant
for the entire congregation.

As congregations welcome new members, recognize Sunday school teachers, commission those going on mission trips, and acknowledge other activities in the life of the congregation, gathering around the font or baptismal space provides the opportunity to connect the ministries of the church with the claims of baptism. Baptism marks and provides the gifts for all Christians to serve together as signs of Christ in the world.

Keeping Our Baptismal Birthright

GENESIS 25:19–34; ROMANS 8:1–11;
MATTHEW 13:1–9, 18–23

As I was leaving town a couple of weeks ago, several of you offered me the same piece of advice: Don't get into trouble. What surprised me is that a week at the Presbyterian General Assembly in Fort Worth and a week at the Lutheran Theological Seminary in Philadelphia are usually not at the top of most lists of hell-raising adventures. Nevertheless, I took your advice to heart and tried to be on my best behavior. I actually avoided trouble from Saturday all the way until Wednesday morning, when I went to listen to biblical scholar Ched Myers.

Ched was leading a Bible study at the peacemaking booth in the exhibit hall at General Assembly. The peacemaking booth is the place where many activists gather, and it was clear that this was no ordinary group. When I walked up to the booth, I discovered about forty people sitting and standing as they waited for the Bible study to begin. There were people of all ages, including several seniors with a long-term commitment to peace and justice causes. We stood there side by side right across from the Presbyterians for Renewal booth, where conservative activists gathered. No more than five feet from us, two dour-looking Presbyterians were handing out pamphlets that among other things called for a return to the Heidelberg Catechism as the path to the future.

Ched began talking to us about the liberating power of the gospel that calls our habits and assumptions into question. He had just returned from London, where thousands of Christians had gathered to form a human chain across the bridges over the Thames River to call for Jubilee 2000—a plan offered by the church to lift the load of debt off the backs of developing nations. Then Ched asked us to talk about what was going on in our communities. People told all kinds of stories of ways that Presbyterians are reaching out to welcome and include our neighbors, strategies from soup kitchens to tutoring centers. I glanced over at the folk in the Presbyterians for Renewal booth; they did not seem too convinced. It was then that someone got the idea that we should sing. So there in the middle of the exhibit booths, we raised our voices and sang a chorus at the top of our lungs: "What's the matter that the church don't shout? The devil's inside and gotta come out. Jubilee! Jubilee! Oh, Lordy, Jubilee."

The witness of these longtime Presbyterians affirmed for me that the church is the place to raise our voices and to call out for a better future, especially on behalf of the many whose voices are not heard. Over and over again, the gospel underscores the message that Jesus did not come to bring spiritual piety and comfortable platitudes, but to challenge us, especially us religious folk, to live out our beliefs in ways that will bring hope to the world.

Through the waters of baptism, we are given a birthright to live as witnesses to the good news that God's grace reaches out to all people. Or, as St. Francis of Assisi is reported to have said: Proclaim the gospel always; use words if necessary. Sometimes it is difficult to remember why this is so important. We get so caught up in our own needs of the moment that we wonder why we even need this birthright anymore. We might as well trade it in for something more valuable. Esau chose bread and lentil stew. After all, he was hungry after a long day in the fields.

This story of Jacob and Esau always seems blatantly unfair to me. Where is Jacob's sense of hospitality and brotherly love? Esau works all day long and comes home exhausted. Why doesn't Jacob simply offer him something to eat? Beyond the puzzles of this story, there is something else going on here. This is a modern-day parable about our desire to fulfill our own needs at any price. If we have to sell our birthright—well, why not? This story challenges us to remember our past and to hang onto it, even as we look to the future. Memory helps us recognize the significance of our birthright, and vision helps us discover how to live out this heritage.

Friends, the birthright of this congregation throughout its history is to raise our voice and reach out to those who are forgotten, alienated, or ignored. It is a legacy that runs back to the days when Reverend Long welcomed black soldiers to sleep in our building because they were discriminated against and excluded from other places.

At times, this birthright will make us uncomfortable. Church is the place where we are expected to behave with decency and order. We put on our good clothes, and we act polite. We pretend that everything is all right in the world and in our own lives, while we desperately hope to hear something that will make sense of our lives. In the eighth chapter of Romans, the apostle Paul reminds us that Christ sets us free from all of the expectations and requirements of the law of religious life so that the Spirit will give birth to something new in us. Through the waters of baptism, the Spirit turns our minds from death toward life and peace.

Keeping our birthright requires vigilance and patience. The Gospel lesson reminds us that the seeds we plant do not all take root, and that they require time to grow. There are days of rain and times of weeding and long periods of waiting. Yet even through the long, dry periods of our lives, there is no reason to panic and sell our birthright. It is a time to wait for the Spirit to deepen our roots and to nourish us and provide for us. Listen to the good news: God welcomes us and accepts us and claims our past as a way to lead us toward a new future.

I spent last week in Philadelphia poring through nineteenth-century texts about the struggle of the Reformed church to maintain its birthright. Once the revivals and sawdust trails of the Great Awakening began to sweep the country, Presbyterians were caught in a dilemma. Should we mimic the culture around us to be successful? As people struggled with this question, one man, John Williamson Nevin, pointed back to our birthright as Reformed Christians who are a part of the holy catholic apostolic church. Nevin wrote that worship is the place for

> a sacramental liturgy; a liturgy not just for the pulpit but for the altar; a liturgy ruled by the spirit of the church year; a liturgy that shall be the natural home of the creeds, end chants, and grand old collects, that have come down to us hallowed by the use of the

Church in past ages; a liturgy to be solemnly transacted by the people.[1]

This is a vision of the church taking its birthright into a new world.

Last Sunday morning, my hosts in Philadelphia took me to church. The day was warm and muggy. As we walked into the old church in Germantown, ceiling fans loudly blew warm air at us. I sat quietly through the service and listened to the sermon. During the offering, bread and wine were brought forward to the table for communion. But the procession did not stop there. Baskets of food were carried up and placed by the table. At first, children carried the baskets, but there was so much food that others joined in, until finally a mountain of food was piled up in the front of the church. Each week the congregation collects food to distribute to food banks in the area. As the children and adults carried the food forward, we sang together: "Taste and see, taste and see, the goodness of the Lord."

That is precisely what church is about. It is the place to come and give thanks for God's grace, and from this place we go out to work for the healing of our world. It is a place to raise our voices and a place from which we reach out in hope.

Friends, I deeply believe that this is our birthright and vision. As we gather here around word, water, and wine, God is shaping us to look beyond our own interests and expectations to discover ways and places in which we are not just feeding ourselves but addressing the hunger within us and around us. Who knows where this journey will lead us? Surely, along the way, we will raise our voices and sing out for justice and peace for all people. To God be the glory. Amen.

CHAPTER 7

The Baptismal Life

ON A WARM SPRING EVENING, my wife and I are sitting out back in our courtyard enjoying a glass of wine as we unwind from a long workday. Manny, our neighbor, calls out to us from the other side of the fence. "Hey, I've got something that I want to show you." We head over to the fence as he disappears inside his house, only to reappear a few minutes later with an old card. He carefully reaches up and hands it over the fence for us to examine. It is a baptismal card on white parchment. A little metal picture of the Madonna and Child is set into the front of the card. Inside is an announcement of his baptism as a young child nearly fifty years ago in a church in Cuba. Recently, one of his relatives found the card and brought it to him. It serves as an iconic memory of the enduring claims of baptism, a reminder that we remain God's beloved children even when we are years or miles away from the places where we were baptized.

The enduring power of baptism is not limited to a moment in time. Instead, the baptismal waters trace across the arc of our lives to mark us as God's own. Christian ethicist Christine Gudorf declares that the sacraments intend "to point our attention and appreciation beyond the ritual itself to the ongoing life processes they imitate."[1] In light of this understanding, it is important to examine the ritual acts of baptism and ask how they picture life. On this point, feminist critiques of baptismal practices have raised significant questions about the ways in which baptismal rites emphasize images of new birth to the neglect of women's role as those who give birth. When male clergy use exclusively masculine language and images, they marginalize the role of women in giving birth to the individual who is seeking baptism.[2] In these situations, Susan Ross, a liturgical theologian, observes, "Women give physical birth, but spiritual birth—'real' birth—is given by male clerics in baptism."[3] This important analysis should prompt a revision of baptismal language that acknowledges the role of women and the gift of each child as a sign of God's grace. Baptism is not an ersatz birth rite. By naming and acknowledging physical birth as God's gift of life, the church links the act of baptism with God's ongoing work of creation. Baptism reaches back in thanksgiving to our births and stretches forward to our deaths. In using the image of new birth, baptism reaffirms God's good work in sustaining creation. The language of new birth in the waters of baptism does not seek to negate the first birth, but to underscore God's redemptive work throughout our lives. The language of baptismal water as the womb of new birth, as well as imagery of God's maternal love and care for us, can provide balance in services that have historically emphasized masculine images to the neglect of feminine language.[4]

Scripture provides insights that affirm the roles and gifts that we bring to the community. The apostle Paul, rarely considered a proto-feminist, recognized that baptism creates a bond uniting Christians in ways that overshadow the many differences that separate us. "As many of you as were baptized into Christ have clothed yourselves with Christ. There is no longer Jew or Greek, there is no longer slave or free, there is no longer male and female; for all of you are one in Christ Jesus" (Gal. 3:27–28). This theological claim does not erase the unique perspectives that we bring to the community, but declares that our unity in Christ supersedes other distinctions. Baptism creates a tie that binds us together despite all other differences.

Baptism unites us not only with one another, but also with all of creation. On a hot August afternoon in Louisville, members of the Sacrament Study Task Force, a group appointed by the Presbyterian Church (USA) to study and reflect on the sacraments, spent the day poring over papers and debating nuances of language as we crafted a response to questions about the relationship between baptism and the Lord's Supper. When it came time for evening prayer, we headed out of the building, across the street, and down toward the public park that runs alongside the Ohio River. There, in a playground around a water fountain that shoots jets of water up out of the ground, we sang and danced and played with children as we publicly reaffirmed our baptismal vows once again. It was there in a water park that the significance of baptismal water from a playground hit me between the eyes. In the park we danced through the water with children whom we had never seen before. There on the banks of the river it was clear that we could no longer separate this group of people from that one, or this part of God's creation from another part. The water we use in baptism is a part of the water in the world around us. As we pass through this water, we take our place in caring for the world around us. The importance of liturgy as that which leads us, confronts us, and shapes us is lifted up alongside the joy of the community that surrounds us and sustains us.

Christian ethicist John Hart connects the ability of baptismal water to evoke images of cleansing and new life with the availability of accessible, unpolluted water in the world. The existence of polluted and privatized water diminishes the power of the ritual to embody God's generosity and graciousness. The presence of living water, clean and available to all, conveys God's goodness and provision in creating a world that sustains life. The use of water in our worship services acknowledges our fundamental dependence on God, who provides us with life and calls us to serve as responsible stewards of creation. The loss of clean, available water is significant for our daily lives as well as our rituals. Hart comments on the ramifications of polluted water for the church in this way:

> Throughout the world today . . . environmental degradation and water privatization have caused water to lose its nature and role as *living water*, as a bountiful source of benefits for the common good. Water is losing also its ability to be a *sacramental* symbol, a sign in nature of God the Creator.[5]

As I write, a large oil spill in the Gulf of Mexico threatens the existence of fish and other sea creatures, marshlands, and the livelihood of vast numbers of people who live along the coastline. This

environmental disaster underscores the need for Christians to engage in practices that will sustain the earth. The water in our sanctuary that we use in baptism is linked to all water on this earth.
Christians carry a special responsibility to work for clean water
that is available to all people. We are connected to and dependent
on the rivers, lakes, and oceans that surround us. Without water to
sustain us, we cannot live. Without water, the practices that have
sustained Christian faith will not last.

When the water in our baptismal pools and fonts cannot be
taken from the rivers, lakes, and ocean around us for fear of
contamination, then the church loses one more vital connection
between worship and the world in which we live. We resort to
actions that are limited to our sanctuaries, and the transformative claims of the gospel on the cosmos are reduced to words and
gestures that are primarily for church insiders. Baptism, begun as
an outdoor activity, a sign of renewal in the world, runs the risk
of becoming a privatized ritual for those who still enter the doors
of our sanctuaries.

Christians have a special role and responsibility to play in caring for and assisting in the efforts to clean up our water sources
and provide potable water for all people. Our care for the water in
creation, water we use in baptism, is directly related to Christian
faith that embraces the world as a sign of God's goodness and
provision.[6] The church's work in this effort provides a baptismal
testimony to our neighbors. When asked why we are spending our
time, energy, and money on caring for the environment, we can
respond that it is because of the importance of water as God's gift
to all people and a sign of God's grace.[7] Hart concludes:

> Appreciation for a sacramental universe and a sacramental com-
> mons, and actions to restore, conserve, and increase the availabili-
> ty of living water for members of the sacramental community, will
> prove invaluable for Christians confronting the worsening water
> crisis. Since living water is one of the most essential components
> of a healthy sacramental and revelatory commons, people of all
> faiths should be especially engaged in efforts to ensure that wa-
> ter is neither polluted nor privatized, and, where either or both
> of these violations of water's integrity have occurred against this
> fluid common good of the commons, which is intended for the

common good of all, to reverse such practices and prevent their recurrence.[8]

Each week, Lutheran pastor Walt Lichtenberger invites members of the suburban congregation he serves to bring water gifts to church to use at the beginning of the service. Families or individuals bring water from home or from places where they have traveled. As the service begins, members of the congregation bring the water they have collected and pour it into the baptismal font, and then the congregation remembers its baptismal vows. The youth group brought water back from a trip to a national youth gathering, and other youth brought water from a band trip to Rome. Families have collected water from the ocean and from nearby lakes. A couple remembered their fiftieth wedding anniversary by offering water from their family cabin, where they had vacationed for years. Water was even poured at a funeral from the backyard pond of the home where the deceased used to fish. This practice has helped the members connect the waters of baptism with their daily lives. It helps them see the water around them in new ways as they recognize how all water represents our baptism.

Water's central role in the world and as a part of Christian worship is evident in the architecture of a small chapel that sits in the woods in Hale County, an impoverished area in Alabama, where the Rural Studio provides a place for architecture students at Auburn University to learn about the social responsibilities of architecture. The immersion program, founded by architect Samuel Mockbee, was developed to model an "architecture of decency" by building homes and gathering spaces for people who exist on limited resources.[9] One of the earliest buildings, the Yancey Chapel, is nestled in the woods. As you walk toward the chapel, you pass between two rows of large iron basins that collect rainwater. The walk to the chapel itself provides an opportunity to remember one's baptism. The walls of the chapel are constructed of a thousand old tires filled with dirt, stacked in place, and covered with stucco. In fact, the chapel is often referred to as "the tire chapel." A small channel in the floor at the base of one wall allows water to run through the building and collect in an area near the pulpit. The preacher walks across the water on small stones to climb the steps to the pulpit. Behind the pulpit, the chapel is open and exposed so that the congregation looks out on the lush foliage of the valley and hills. The greenness of the surroundings is sustained by God's gift of rain, even as our baptismal lives are sustained by the living water that runs alongside the pews on which we sit.

There is much to admire and learn from the practices and commitments of the Rural Studio. This small chapel shines as a beacon of hope in a community that continues to struggle with injustice, discrimination, and poverty. Charles Reeve describes the work: "In this context, the Rural Studio's glowing jewels are like lighthouses, guiding us past the shoals of indifference and pointing the way to a future of hope."[10] This notion that light serves as a beacon of hope in the world is ancient, one that Jews and Christians have used throughout our history. From its use in the Psalms, where God's word is depicted as light for our path, to Jesus's teaching to the disciples that we are to be the light of the world, the symbolism of light offers a compelling metaphor for our lives. While water is central to baptism, our rite also adopts light as a primary way of embodying the call to the life of discipleship. Following the baptism, a candle is lit from the paschal candle and given to the baptized with the following words:

> Receive the light of Christ;
> you have passed from darkness to light.

To which the people respond:

> You have been enlightened by Christ.
> Walk always as children of the light.[11]

This call to live as light in the world is a call to work for justice even as we are shaped and formed by word and water, bread and wine. Doing justice with a sacramental heart is a response to God's faithful presence in our lives and an invitation to live out of that presence in the world. Or, in the words of the African American spiritual, we respond to God's goodness that bathes us in the light of grace:

> Shine on me, shine on me.
> Let the light from the lighthouse shine on me.[12]

A Journey for a Lifetime

The image of baptism as a source of light in our lives and in the world is a metaphor for the primary image of journey that we have explored throughout this book. As we have seen, the New Testament provides a vast array of associations with baptism—washing, cleansing, repentance, healing, dying, rising, new birth, Spirit, anointing, and adoption, to name but a few. All of these images are subsumed in one tapestry, that of baptism as a lifelong journey of call, discernment, and service. Scripture presents this meta-narrative in the life of Christ. The Gospels portray Jesus's baptism by John the Baptist in the Jordan River as the defining moment in his preparation for his public ministry of healing, feeding, teaching, and preaching the good news of God's reign. In his two-volume historical survey of baptismal rites, Bryan Spinks notes that "both historically and theologically all baptismal rituals look back to the baptism of Jesus in the Jordan."[13]

What remains striking and curious is how this Jewish renewal ritual became an essential practice in widely diverse Christian communities over the course of two thousand years. Jesus's baptism leads to a time of vocational discernment that defines his public ministry. The Gospel writers recount the story of Jesus's baptism as a way of articulating a call to ministry. The journey of discipleship and the road to the cross are presented as an ongoing baptismal narrative, a story of baptism into death. In Mark's Gospel, for example, Jesus asks his disciples, "Are you able to drink the cup that I drink, or be baptized with the baptism that I am baptized with?" (Mark 10:38). The linking of baptism with Jesus's ministry of self-giving provides the interpretive clue to the church's adoption of baptism as a ritual that moves beyond a simple initiation rite. The apostle Paul provides the essential theological foundation for this transformation as he describes baptism as the process of taking on the cruciform shape of Christ's life. "Therefore we have been buried with him by baptism into death, so that, just as Christ was raised from the dead by the glory of the Father, so we too might walk in newness of life" (Rom. 6:4).

In baptism, the Christ story is enacted on us. The proclamation of the gospel, of Jesus's presentation of the reign of God, is an invitation to all people to respond to Jesus's words: "Come and follow me." As we have discovered, this invitation is a call to live into this new way of life together as a community. The church invites newcomers to learn about this way of life together by preparing for baptism as the church reaches out to serve those who are poor, forgotten, and marginalized. The church celebrates with those who are being baptized the cruciform shape that our lives take as disciples. The church journeys and toils together in the promise that God is resurrecting us and our world. Like the journeys of ancient Israelites who traveled through the Red Sea and escaped from slavery to travel to the promised land, our journey through the waters of baptism is one of hope that God's reign is coming.

According to Lee Hartmann, baptism is the door into a new community:

> But this community is on a journey to a promised land. The ritual of baptism expresses some dimensions of the journey—rebirth, and from death to life. It is a journey with the risen Lord Jesus Christ, which he began in the incarnation, but publicly launched at the baptism in the Jordan and concluded in the *baptisma* on the Cross, and beyond in eternity.[14]

A primary goal of worship renewal is to recover baptism as a lifelong journey in which our lives take on the sign of Christ. From this perspective, the sacraments of baptism and Eucharist can no longer be confined within the walls of our sanctuaries. Instead, the church uses water, bread, and wine—each a part of creation—to declare our status as beloved sons and daughters of God. This incredible good news prompts us to work for peace and justice and the redemption of the world that God created and declared as good.

Baptism as Witness

One school year, at the first meeting of the seminar I teach on baptism, I spoke with the students about a new class assignment. I required each of them to go to their own congregations and interview ten people about their memories and understanding of baptism. The goal of the exercise was to bring the experiences of our congregations' members into dialogue with the readings and experiences in our classroom. I was surprised to encounter reluctance from the students to do the assignment. The following weekend I was at a seminar for seminary teachers and described the class reaction to one of my peers. She asked me if I had done any of the interviews. When I said I had not, she challenged me to try it. So the next Sunday, I stood up during the announcements and invited people in our small congregation to talk with me about their baptismal memories after the service. To my amazement, people lined up down the center aisle to describe their experiences to me. One of the most memorable interviews was with a woman who spoke of her children's baptism in our church after she had moved to Richmond.

> I have two children who were baptized here. My daughter was baptized here. I was a student on campus when I came here. After I married in Richmond, I came here. They used to sprinkle right there in front at church.
>
> I dressed them up in white. There were eleven years between our children. My son was baptized earlier than the girl. He was still a baby—less than a year.
>
> Baptism always has been a joyous occasion.
>
> Now my daughter is deceased. She was buried in this church. She became a minister. She died in 2002. I brought her back here to be buried where she was baptized.[15]

Her experience is a living witness to the language of a prayer in the funeral rite, a service of witness to the resurrection:

> *Especially we thank you for your servant N.,*
> *Whose baptism is now complete in death.*
> *We praise you for his/her life,*
> *For all in him/her that was good and kind and faithful,*
> *For the grace you gave him/her,*
> *That kindled in him/her the love of your dear name,*
> *And enabled him/her to serve you faithfully.[16]*

This is the witness of the baptismal life. From our inception, even as our mothers carry us in the fluids of their wombs, until our bodies are returned to the earth, our lives are a journey toward hope. The One who breathes life into us at our birth and creates us in God's own image places us on this good earth to live together and to take part in the dance of life. Our brief time on this earth is a journey of living into the promise of baptism, where we are welcomed into a community of faith as God's beloved children. From the baptismal water, we move in hope toward God's reign by practicing hospitality, caring for creation, and providing food, shelter, and healing to those in need. This baptismal life, this water journey that we share, is an adventure as we move together into God's future.

This vision of promise and hope is what worship leaders hold before the congregation each week as we gather for worship. Leading parts of the service from the baptismal space keeps the vows of baptism before us on a regular basis. Some denominations and congregations are reclaiming practices that reinforce the dramatic promises of baptism on our lives.[17] In the Reformation, Martin Luther declared that when his faith wavered he remembered, "I am baptized." Likewise, Martin Bucer, the Reformed pastor, advocated that every worship service should begin with a confession of sin, because the Christian life begins at the time of baptism.[18] For Bucer, the ongoing practice of confession grew out of the initial profession of faith in baptism.

Worship leaders can build on the theological foundation of baptism's central place in the Christian life by keeping baptismal imagery and practices central in worship each week. Pouring water and using language replete with baptismal imagery reinforces the connection of baptism with our daily lives. For example, worship services that include commissioning Sunday school teachers or youth groups that are preparing for mission trips can show that these forms of service are an outgrowth of our baptisms. Simple language and gesture are all that is needed. We might pour water into a bowl and state that we gather here to celebrate this occasion because in our baptism the Spirit gives us gifts for ministry and service. Regular use of baptismal language and images avoids relegating baptism to one moment in time.

Scripture paints a vision of this future in the final chapter of the book of Revelation. The depiction draws heavily on the imagery of the creation narratives in Genesis, where God separates the earth from the waters of the firmament. There the Spirit moves across the water and breathes life into all living things. After each step of creation, God looks around and declares it good. The author of Revelation brings back the imagery from Eden:

> Then the angel showed me the river of the water of life, bright as crystal, flowing from the throne of God and of the Lamb through the middle of the street of the city. On either side of the river is the tree of life with its twelve kinds of fruit, producing its fruit each month; and the leaves of the tree are for the healing of the nations.
>
> —Revelation 22:1–2

In his commentary on this passage, New Testament scholar Brian Blount observes, "The river marks the city as a new, improved, urban Eden. John builds his case carefully. He notes that the river is composed of living water. As such, it is a metaphor for the gift of eschatological relationship with God that humans experienced before their expulsion from paradise. They have thirsted for its restoration ever since."[19] This vision of a new heaven and earth springs up from the water that God provides. In this new place, the water provides for the healing of the nations. The words of the gospel song sum up this hope:

> *O healing river, send down your waters*
> *Send down your waters upon this land.*[20]

In John's vision, the living water is the source for the healing of the nations. It also nourishes the fruit of the trees that provide sustenance for all who dwell in this new creation. Here the imagery of the waters of baptism in the river of life is linked to the food from the tree of life that we will share together. Baptism and Eucharist are held together in one scene as the source and summit of new life. Thus, baptism offers us a vision of new life shared in and for the community and sustained by the gifts of bread and wine as we gather around the table.

MEDITATION 7

Water and Bread

Acts 27:27–36

"This road differs from those on dry land in three ways. The one on land is firm, this unstable. The one on land is quiet, this moving. The one on land is marked, the one on the sea, unknown."[1] These words come from the sixteenth-century Spanish cartographer Martin Cortes de Albacar, whose book *The Art of Navigation* was the first manual of any type printed in the English language. Cortes's work provided a guide to the difficult task of crossing the seas. As we gather here this morning to reflect on worship renewal, I want to talk with you about how our worship shapes the way we interpret Scripture.

Our passage from the book of Acts is a brief portion of a longer travelogue of Paul's journey by sea to Rome. Paul was under arrest and being transported to Rome to stand trial. It was early fall, and the Mediterranean is often turbulent at that time of year. Paul and the other prisoners were transferred to a ship out of Alexandria that was headed to Italy, but as they neared Crete, the storms rolled in, and the ship was in danger. The wind became so strong and the sea so rough that finally, in an act of desperation, the crew of the ship began to throw the ship's cargo overboard. Paul tells us, "When neither sun nor stars appeared for many days, and no small tempest raged, all hope of our being saved was at last abandoned" (Acts 27:20).

At this moment, Paul, the hero of our adventure, who was never known for being soft-spoken, steps onstage. His speech can be summed up in four simple words: "I told you so." I told you that we should never have left Crete and headed out on this adventure.

But now comes the good news: Paul declares that God will grant safety to the shipmates on their journey. "So keep up your courage." Paul's speech is a brave and inspiring performance. Yet in today's Scripture passage, we find the ship several days later drifting across the sea and dodging rocks, and the sailors trying to escape to save their own lives. And so our hero Paul intervenes for a second time. He calls the crew members together and tells them that they must stay together to be saved.

I am drawn to this sea yarn from the book of Acts because Paul's work and ministry in the church are presented in the form of a journey. Tossed around amid dangerous waves, Paul and the sailors are cast as characters in a tale of grit, faith, and survival. It is an imperfect and perhaps uncomfortable analogy for life in the church, and yet one that seems fitting when we consider the challenges that congregations face in a changing world. Amid economic crises and environmental disasters, the church can become a safe haven, a place of comfort while turbulent winds are whipping around us. The gospel message does not call us to abandon the world. Rather it equips us to carry a word of hope on our baptismal journey—this water voyage. This morning as we consider your congregation's call to serve in the world, I offer you the words of that other Paul: "I urge you now to keep up your courage, have faith in God" (vs. 25).

In the face of adversity, another pep talk is not enough. Paul gathers the crew and the prisoners around him and tells them that it is time to eat. They have gone fourteen days without food, and they are exhausted and discouraged. So Paul takes bread and gives thanks to God and breaks it and begins to eat. "Then all of them were encouraged and took food for themselves" (vs. 36). It sounds like a pretty straightforward passage. But you probably noticed that Luke uses the same vocabulary here as he uses at the Last Supper: of taking bread, giving thanks (*eucharistein*—the Greek word for thanksgiving), breaking bread, and eating. When I read this story, it sounds as though worship renewal is taking place on board this ship. Here is precisely where reading and interpreting this text can get tricky. The way we worship shapes the way we understand this text. For example, listen to the way a couple of biblical scholars offer differing perspectives on this passage.

New Testament scholar Hans Conzelmann's comments: "This is not a reference to a celebration of the Eucharist. The scene describes the way that Christians customarily eat."[2] Here Conzelmann assumes that the way Christians eat has nothing to do with communion. While his own experience may not have prepared him to see the connections, worship renewal teaches us to expect the presence of the risen Christ every time and place we gather to break bread. When all our meals become occasions for thanksgiving, then we see in this reading from Acts a remarkable moment in which Paul and all those around him unexpectedly encounter God's grace.

Beverly Gaventa, another New Testament scholar, argues that because there is no mention of wine and no explicit description of Paul himself handing out the bread, it doesn't really count as a eucharistic meal. She is also concerned about what she identifies as the problem of a communion service in which Christians share their food with all those pagans.[3] Once again, our focus on worship renewal can help us see this text in a different light. When we welcome everyone—church members, guests, and strangers—to this table, we begin to see ourselves in light of Paul's actions in this text. He takes bread—whatever he can get his hands on—and in a spirit of thanksgiving offers it not simply to his friends, but to all who are there.

This text is modeling a new way of life for us together. Paul urges *all* those on the ship to partake of the food for their own salvation (*sotereia,* for you Greek scholars out there). In a striking parallel of Jesus's actions at the meal in Emmaus in Luke 24, Paul takes the bread, gives thanks to God, breaks it, and begins to eat. And *all* took heart and partook of the food.[4]

This morning I offer you this text as a model for the worship that you are doing here. In this community, you are surrounded by people who simply long to hear a word of hope and to be fed. There are times when you will have to decide whether to respond to the needs of those around you or to do things the way that they have always been done. On those occasions, I hope you will recall this text in which hospitality even to one's captors and generosity toward all become the signs of the community that forms on board this ship. Speaking a word of encouragement, extending an open

invitation, giving thanks to God, and breaking bread and sharing it with all—these are the actions of faithful disciples of Jesus
Christ.

Friends, we go out from this place to travel a different path.
This water way—this baptismal journey—is unstable, moving,
and unmarked. Yet we do not travel this way alone. The night
stars that shine down upon us are the same stars that twinkled
in the sky above Paul and others who have gone before us. With
Christ as our compass, we will make it through the storms of life
safely to the other side. Along the way, whenever possible, take
bread, give thanks to God, break it, and share it with *all*. To God
be the glory. Amen.

NOTES

CHAPTER 1: LOOKING FOR WATER?

1. *Baptism, Eucharist and Ministry* (Geneva: World Council of Churches, 1982), 3.

2. *Evangelical Lutheran Worship* (Minneapolis: Augsburg Fortress, 2006), 229. It is worth noting that denominational worship books will phrase these questions in slightly different terms as ways of expressing theological nuances that are important to particular denominations.

3. E.g., Do you believe in God, the Father almighty?

4. Rudolf Bultmann, *Jesus Christ and Mythology* (New York: Charles Scribner's Sons, 1958), 17.

5. Bultmann, *Jesus Christ and Mythology,* 36 and 40.

6. The citation of this passage in a book on baptism requires commentary about the way that this text in particular has been misappropriated as grounds for the practice of infant baptism. While there may well be solid biblical and theological grounds for infant baptism, proof-texting with this passage surely is not an effective argument. For more on this issue, see John Calvin, *Institutes of Christian Religion*, vol. 2 (Grand Rapids: Eerdmans, 1979), 533. Note Karen Spierling's analysis in *Infant Baptism in Reformation Geneva* (Louisville: Westminster John Knox, 2005), 56.

7. Paul Tillich, *Dynamics of Faith* (New York: Harper & Row, 1959), 18ff.

8. Ludwig Wittgenstein, *On Certainty* (Oxford, England: Basil Blackwell, 1979), 28e.

MEDITATION 1: BAPTISMAL INGREDIENTS

1. William Wordsworth, "Ode: Intimations of Immortality," *Recollections of Early Childhood* (Whitefish, Montana: Kessinger Publishing, LLC, 2010), 15.

CHAPTER 2: INQUIRY

1. From *The Greek Life of Pachomius*, quoted in Alan Kreider, *The Change of Conversion and the Origin of Christendom* (Harrisburg, Pa.: Trinity Press, 1999), 19.

2. Since communion was reserved for the baptized, newcomers would be allowed to participate in only part of the service.

3. Bard Thompson, ed., "The First Apology of Justin Martyr," *Liturgies of the Western Church* (New York: New American Library, 1961), 9.

4. Justin Martyr in Thompson, ed., "The First Apology," 9.

5. Justin Martyr in Kreider, *The Change of Conversion*, 5.

6. Octavius in Kreider, *The Change of Conversion*, 19.

7. For example, the directory for worship in the former Southern Presbyterian Church did not even recognize the possibility of an adult baptism. The close alliance of church and culture expected that being a good Christian was the result of being born in a Christian home and nurtured by a Christian culture.

8. See the official website of the MST: http://www.mstbrazil.org/.

9. Reynolds Price in Barbara Brown Taylor, "He Who Fills All in All," *Home by Another Way* (Cambridge, Mass.: Cowley Publications, 1999), 138.

10. This portrait is adapted from Cláudio Carvalhaes and Paul Galbreath, "The Season of Easter: Imaginative Figurings for the Body of Christ," *Interpretation*, January 2011.

MEDITATION 2: BIRTH PANGS

1. *Book of Common Worship* (Louisville: Westminster John Knox, 1993), 412.

2. Anthony Robinson, "Renewed Life," *The Christian Century* 117, no. 32 (November 15, 2000): 1184.

CHAPTER 3: COMPANIONS

1. Years ago when I was in graduate school, my conservative Christian roommate reported to me that someone had knocked on our apartment door seeking donations to a Christian children's fund. When he tried to determine the legitimacy of the group, he fell back on the questions taught him by his own congregation. "Do you believe in the virgin birth?" he asked. When the individual answered in the affirmative, my roommate promptly donated twenty dollars. As it turned out, the donation went to support the work of the Rev. Sun Myung Moon, not exactly what my roommate had in mind.

2. Daniel T. Benedict, *Come to the Waters* (Nashville: Discipleship Resources, 1996), 10. "The sequence and elements of this story and others in the Book of Acts illustrate the logic and flow of evangelization, conversion, formation, and initiation that developed in the early centuries of the church."

3. Frederick Buechner, *Beyond Words: Daily Readings in the ABC's of Faith* (San Francisco: Harper Collins, 2004), 14.

4. This approach was prompted by Ched Myers, whose commentary on the Gospel of Mark, *Binding the Strong Man* (Maryknoll, N.Y.: Orbis Books, 1990) broke new interpretive ground.

5. Tom Long, *The Witness of Preaching* (Louisville: Westminster John Knox, 1989), 44–45.

6. Apostolic Traditions, 10.

7. Alan Kreider, *The Change of Conversion and the Origin of Christendom* (Harrisburg, Pa.: Trinity Press, 1999), 8–9.

8. Kreider, *The Change of Conversion*, 9.

9. See the discussion of Constantine's conversion in Kreider, *The Change of Conversion*, 33ff. Only at the end of his life did Constantine seek baptism when he decided to eschew signs of wealth. Eusebius reported that Constantine "resolved never to come in contact with purple again" (p. 37).

10. Kreider, *The Change of Conversion*, 67.

11. Kreider, *The Change of Conversion*, 67.

12. Kreider, *The Change of Conversion*, 69.

13. Crafting revisionist history, Christian conservatives attempt to impose Judeo-Christian values on the broader culture in the United States by posting the Ten Commandments in public places or claiming the founding fathers as evangelical siblings. These attempts bypass the deeper vision of baptismal formation that is central to the vision of Christian identity and practice that we are exploring.

MEDITATION 3: DIRTY WATER, DUSTY FEET

1. Henry Purcell, "When I Am Laid in Earth," from the opera *Dido and Aeneus*.

CHAPTER 4: RENUNCIATION

1. *Book of Common Worship* (Louisville: Westminster John Knox, 1993), 407.

2. The earliest record of these questions is from Tertullian. In *De corona*, iii, he writes, "When we are going to enter the water, but a little before, in the presence of the congregation and under the hand of the president, we solemnly profess that we disown the devil, and his pomp, and his angels" (Tertullian in W. Caspari, "The Renunciation of the Devil in the Baptismal Rite," *The New Schaff-Herzog Encyclopedia of Religious Knowledge,* vol. IX, ed. Samuel Macauley Jackson [Grand Rapids: Baker Book House, 1953], 489; http://www.ccel.org/s/schaff/encyc/encyc09/htm/iv.vii.clxiii.htm). In the third-century manuscript The Canons of Hipolytus, an explicit liturgical formula is provided: "The catechumen turned to the West (symbolically the region of darkness) and repeated: 'I renounce thee, Satan, with all thy pomp.'"

3. Zwingli and Calvin eliminated the renunciations in their baptismal rites, and the renunciations increasingly came under scrutiny by rationalists in the nineteenth century. The return of some version of the renunciations is in part a result of the work of ecumenical liturgical movement.

4. See baptismal rites in Thomas F. Best, ed., *Baptism Today* (Collegeville, Minn.: Liturgical Press, 2008).

5. From the Roman Catholic baptismal rite in *Baptism Today,* 331.

6. Presbyterian Church of Canada, http://www.leasidepresbyterianchurch.ca/baptismra.htm.

7. Following the work of Victor Turner, ritual scholars use "liminality" to describe the ritual acts of transition. Liminal actions are those that place individuals in a new place in the life of the community.

8. *Common Order* (Edinburgh: Saint Andrew Press, 1996), 102. See *Call to Worship* 39, no. 4: 8; note 16 as well.

9. Ched Myers, Marie Dennis, Joseph Nangle, OFM, Cynthia Moe-Lobeda, Stuart Taylor, *"Say to This Mountain": Mark's Story of Discipleship* (Maryknoll, N.Y.: Orbis Books, 1996), 126.

10. Chris von Allsburg, *The Wretched Stone* (New York: Houghton Mifflin, 1991).

11. See Douglas R. A. Hare, *Matthew* (Louisville: John Knox, 1993), 24–25.

12. Gordon Mikoski, *Baptism and Christian Identity: Teaching in the Triune Name* (Grand Rapids: Eerdmans, 2009), 36.

13. C. K. Barrett, *Church Ministry and Sacraments in the New Testament* (Grand Rapids: Eerdmans, 1985), 69.

14. In his summary of New Testament foundations for baptism, Bryan Spinks concludes, "The books of the New Testament present neither a single doctrine of baptism, nor some archetypal liturgical rite. The various writers allude to baptism, or discuss baptism in passing, or are concerned to draw out Christological and salvific claims from the fact of Jesus' baptism, but beyond that we have not so much a systematic baptismal theology as some kaleidoscopic pictures" (Spinks, *Early and Medieval Rituals and Theologies of Baptism* [Aldershot, England: Ashgate, 2006], 12–13).

15. Karl Gerlach, *The Antenicene Pascha: A Rhetorical History* (Leuven, Belgium: Peeters Publishers, 1998), 405ff.

16. Dirk Lange, "Gathering, Ordo, and Baptism," *Ordo: Bath, Word, Prayer, Table* (Akron, Ohio: OSL Publications, 2005), 52.

17. Lange, "Gathering, Ordo, and Baptism," 53.

MEDITATION 4: WHEN THE SPIRIT MOVES

1. Marty Haugen's adaptation of Isaiah 12:3, "With Joy You Shall Draw Water" (Chicago: GIA Publications, 1988).

CHAPTER 5: WATER

1. My thanks to Cláudio Carvalhaes for leading this service in Lake Chapel at Union Presbyterian Seminary in Richmond, Virginia.

2. *The Land and the Sacred: Nature's Role in Myth and Religion*, vol. 2, *Water and Its Powers* (Princeton, N.J.: Films for the Humanities and Sciences).

3. Philip Larkin, "Water," *The Whitsun Weddings* (London: Faber & Faber, 1975).

4. For the description of parallels between Qumran and early Christian baptismal practice, see Ben Witherington III, *Troubled Waters: Rethinking the Theology of Baptism* (Waco, Texas: Baylor University Press, 2007), 22–24.

5. It is worth noting, though, that the most significant ecumenical work on baptism in our time, *Baptism, Eucharist and Ministry*, fails to even mention the biblical variations in baptismal formulas (*Baptism, Eucharist and Ministry*, Faith and Order Paper No. 111 [Geneva: World Council of Churches, 1982], 6).

6. From "The Didache" in James White, *Documents of Christian Worship* (Louisville: Westminster John Knox, 1992), 147.

7. Paul F. Bradshaw, *Eucharistic Origins* (Oxford, England: Oxford University Press, 2004), 59. Bradshaw cites evidence that includes the following foods: oil, bread, vegetables, salt, cheese, and milk and honey.

8. Andrea Bieler and Luise Schottroff, *The Eucharist: Bread, Bodies, and Resurrection* (Minneapolis: Fortress, 2007), 115. It is worth noting that the passing of a rule does not necessarily mean that all communities immediately followed it!

9. Bryan D. Spinks, *Early and Medieval Rituals and Theologies of Baptism: From the New Testament to the Council of Trent* (Aldershot, England: Ashgate, 2006), 12.

10. Spinks, *Early and Medieval Rituals*, 35–36.

11. Kreider, *The Change of Conversion*, 37.

12. Augustine in Kreider, *The Change of Conversion*, 59: "You in particular, you bad procrastinator with your bad longing for tomorrow, listen to the Lord speaking, listen to holy scripture speaking. . . . 'Do not be slow to turn to the Lord, nor put it off from day to day. For suddenly his wrath will come, and at the time for vengeance he will destroy you.'"

13. Kreider, *The Change of Conversion*, 75.

14. Spinks, *Early and Medieval Rituals*, 66.

15. Daniel Stevick notes that the transition is prompted by factors including the church's move to colder climates where "Roman virtuosity with water was lost. Baptism came to be performed over a bowl which stood on a pedestal in or near the Eucharistic room. Baptism was performed essentially privately, when the child was a few days old" (Stevick, "Baptism, Modes of Administering," *The New Dictionary of Sacramental Worship;* ed. Peter E. Fink, S.J. [Collegeville, Minn.: Liturgical Press, 1990], 107).

16. Karen Spierling, *Infant Baptism in Reformation Geneva* (Louisville: Westminster John Knox, 2005), 102–103.

17. *Baptism, Eucharist and Ministry*, 6–7.

18. Gordon Lathrop, *Holy People: A Liturgical Ecclesiology* (Minneapolis: Fortress, 1999), 138.

19. Note, for example, the commentary provided in the development of a new baptismal rite for the Presbyterian Church (U.S.A.):

Today we live in a secular society in which Christianity is waning in influence and adherents. Those "outside" the church cannot always identify characteristics of Christian living among the baptized that distinguish the baptized from the non-baptized. It is entirely possible that the crisis of the church is really not qualitatively different from the baptismal crisis. The crisis of faith in which belief seems impossible, untenable, or irrelevant may be due in part to the fact that the baptismal realities of belonging to God, being transformed, dying, rising, being joined inextricably to a body of people whose lives are inextricably different are sadly "invisible realities." Yet they are the ones which baptism and confirmation proclaim and of which they are themselves signs. The first step in addressing that crisis is to begin at the beginning, with a rite whose words and actions correspond more accurately and powerfully with the realities they describe (*Holy Baptism and Services for the Renewal of Baptism, Supplemental Liturgical Resource 2* [Philadelphia: Westminster Press, 1985], 20–21).

20. *Evangelical Lutheran Worship* (Minneapolis: Augsburg Fortress, 2006), 307.

MEDITATION 5: KEEPING THE RIGHT WARDROBE

1. *Book of Common Worship* (Louisville: Westminster John Knox, 1993), 197.

CHAPTER 6: GIFTS

1. *Book of Common Worship*, 413.
2. S. Scott Bartchy, "Undermining Ancient Patriarchy: The Apostle Paul's Vision of a Society of Siblings," *Biblical Theology Bulletin* 29, no. 2:69.
3. Bartchy, "Undermining Ancient Patriarchy," 77.
4. http://www.dalitchristians.com/html/CasteChurch.htm. My thanks to Martha Moore-Keish for describing this predicament to me. When visiting churches in India, she observed that many Dalits are regular participants in congregations but delay baptism because of the drastic financial and cultural ramifications.
5. http://www.aina.org/news/20090616174946.htm.
6. Phillip Jenkins, "The Crypto-Christians," *The Christian Century* 126, no. 14 (July 14, 2009): 45. Thanks to my colleague Stan Skreslet for suggestions in this area.
7. *Book of Common Worship*, 414.
8. Spierling, *Infant Baptism*, 33.
9. John Riggs, *Baptism in the Reformed Tradition: An Historical and Practical Theology* (Louisville: Westminster John Knox, 2002), 113. Riggs offers a critique of the baptismal rite of the *Book of Common Worship*, which he faults for its overreliance on the patterns of Christian initiation from the patristic era and argues for a thorough reexamination of the baptismal rite through the primary lens of covenantal theology. I am in agreement with his critique of the Profession of Faith that it should "open with divine proclamation that the one to be baptized is already a beloved child, *prior to* the baptism" (p. 116). What is missing in Riggs's critique is an understanding that the model of Christian initiation takes its cue from the way that our lives continue to be patterned in the image of Christ. The christological center that Riggs longs to see is operative in the invitation to all to join with us in patterning our lives after Christ.
10. Fikret Yurgel, *Baths and Bathing in Classical Antiquity* (Cambridge, Mass.: MIT Press, 1992), 355; in Spinks, *Early and Medieval Rituals,* vol. 1, 36.
11. "Anointing," *The New Dictionary of Sacramental Worship*, 51.
12. From The Disdacalia, in Spinks, *Early and Medieval Rituals*, 19.
13. Spinks, *Early and Medieval Rituals*, 19.
14. Spinks, *Early and Medieval Rituals*, 36.
15. In *The New Dictionary of Sacramental Worship*, 51.
16. *New Dictionary,* p. 52.
17. Paul Meyendorff provides a helpful analysis of the way that Western Christians are increasingly open to the use of material symbols in our rituals. He concludes by asking the questions: "Does the greater acceptance of symbol and

ritual reflect, in fact, a more positive approach to creation? Or is it simply making the rites more colorful, less stark and boring?" (Meyendorff, "Toward Mutual Recognition of Baptism," in *Baptism Today: Understanding, Practice, Ecumenical Implications*, ed. Thomas F. Best [Collegeville, Minn.: Liturgical Press, 2008], 199).

18. For example, Hughes Oliphant Old comments about the practice of exorcism in sixteenth-century baptismal services: "Once all those exorcisms were translated into German and everybody understood that what you had was twenty minutes of exorcism and three minutes of baptism, it became clear something had to be done" (Old, "Origins of the Reformed Baptismal Rites in the Sixteenth Century," *Reformed Liturgy & Music* 19, no. 4 [Fall 1985]: 197–198).

19. For example, the rubrics in the *Book of Common Worship* include this as an option: "The minister may mark the sign of the cross on the forehead of each of the newly baptized, while saying one of the following. Oil prepared for this purpose may be used" (*BCW*, 413). The rubrics in the *United Methodist Book of Worship* (Nashville: United Methodist Publishing House, 1992), 91, are particularly instructive:

Olive oil may be used in this action, following the biblical custom anointing prophets (I Kings 9:16), priests (Exodus 29:7), and kings (I Kings 1:39). Jesus's titles Christ and Messiah both mean "Anointed One," and the New Testament repeatedly calls Christ our High Priest and King. Christians in baptism become members of the body of Christ (I Corinthians 12:13) which is a "royal priesthood" (I Peter 2:9). Anointing at baptism is a reminder that all Christians are anointed into this royal priesthood.

20. *Book of Common Worship*, 414.

21. Gerlach, *The Antenicene Pascha*, 405ff.

22. A few recent attempts have picked up on this historic connection between Lent and baptism. See Stanley R. Hall, "Becoming Christian: Ash Wednesday and the Sign of Ashes: A Reflection on the Ash Wednesday Liturgy at Austin Theological Seminary," *Reformed Liturgy & Music* 32, no. 4 (1998): 191–195, and Paul Galbreath, *Ash Wednesday: A Three Act Play in Turning, Nurturing, and Growing*, unpublished liturgy for Union Presbyterian Seminary Chapel, 2010.

23. Alternative scriptural passages could include Matthew 5:14–16 or Galatians 5:22–23.

24. Note the ways that this passage has usually been misinterpreted as that which Christians do in order to share some of what we have with "the least of these." The point of the text is not for us to feel noble because we occasionally reach out to those who are below us. The point is that much to our surprise, we discover Christ in these situations as we serve those who are forgotten. See Paul Galbreath, *Leading from the Table* (Herndon, Va.: Alban Institute, 2008), 30–31.

25. *Book of Occasional Services* (Louisville: Geneva Press, 1999), 11.

MEDITATION 6: KEEPING OUR BAPTISMAL BIRTHRIGHT

1. John Williamson Nevin, source unknown.

CHAPTER 7: THE BAPTISMAL LIFE

1. Christine Gudorf in Susan Ross, *Extravagant Affections: A Feminist Sacramental Theology* (New York: Continuum, 1998), 193.
2. While many newer baptismal rites incorporate feminine images (e.g., the font as a womb of new birth), there remains the problem of male presiders usurping female images and roles. As a first step, baptismal rites need to include recognition and thanksgiving for the mother who gave birth and for the individual who already comes to baptism as a gift of God.
3. Ross, *Extravagant Affections,* 193.
4. Here note the baptismal formula developed by Riverside Church in New York City that preserves the historic language while adding feminine imagery: "I baptize you in the name of the Father, the Son, and the Holy Spirit, one God, Mother of us all."
5. John Hart, *Sacramental Commons: Christian Ecological Ethics* (Lanham, Md.: Rowman & Littlefield Publishers, Inc., 2008), 91.
6. This is a particularly important claim for Christians to make. Western, fundamentalist Christians often plunder or ignore the earth's resources, since the imminent return of Christ makes care for the environment unnecessary. Recently, mainline Christians have grown in our awareness of the responsibility that we carry as stewards of creation. Relating this understanding to baptism provides a significant opportunity for us to connect worship practices with our daily lives and practices. In this sense, Christian practices refuse to acknowledge a separation between the physical and spiritual. From this perspective, the use of water in baptism and its role in the world shows the integral link between our physical and spiritual reliance on water. This provides an important contrast to the purification rites of some other faiths, such as the Hindu understanding that washing in the Ganges River provides a spiritual cleansing regardless of the level of contamination of the water.
7. Similar arguments should be made in regard to providing basic food and drink, eucharistic symbols that are available to all people.
8. Hart, *Sacramental Commons,* 93.
9. For more on the Rural Studio, see Andrea Oppenheimer Dean, *Rural Studio: Samuel Mockbee and Architecture of Decency* (New York: Princeton Architectural Press, 2002). I have written about the Rural Studio as a metaphor for the work of the church in "Doing Justice with a Sacramental Heart," *Hungry Hearts* 14, no. 3 (fall 2005).
10. Charles Reeve, "Adrift near the Shoals of Indifference" in David Moos and Gail Trechsel, eds., *Samuel Mockbee and the Rural Studio: Community Architecture* (New York: Distributed Art Publishers, 2003).
11. *Book of Common Worship,* 428.
12. "Shine on Me," *African American Heritage Hymnal* (Chicago: GIA Publications, 2001), 527.
13. Lee Hartmann in Bryan D. Spinks, *Reformation and Modern Rituals and Theologies of Baptism: From Luther to Contemporary Practices* (Hants, England: Ashgate, 2006), 200.
14. Lee Hartmann in Spinks, *Reformation and Modern Rituals and Theologies of Baptism,* 211.
15. Interview with Eleanor Binford.

16. *Book of Common Worship*, 921.

17. See the report of the Sacrament Study Task Force of the PCUSA, "Invitation to Christ," http://www.pcusa.org/sacraments/.

18. Hughes Oliphant Olds, "Origins of the Reformed Baptismal Rites in the Sixteenth Century," *Reformed Liturgy & Music* 19, no. 4 (fall 1985): 200.

19. Brian Blount, *Revelation: A Commentary* (Louisville: Westminster John Knox, 2009), 395.

20. Fred Hellerman and Fran Minkoff, "Healing River," *Gather Comprehensive* (Chicago: GIA Publications, 2004), no. 584.

MEDITATION 7: WATER AND BREAD

1. Martin Cortes de Albacar in Arturo Perez-Reverte, *The Nautical Chart*, trans. Margaret Sayers Peden (New York: Mariner Books, 2004), 326.

2. Hanz Conzelmann, *Acts of the Apostles* (Philadelphia: Fortress, 1987), 220.

3. Beverly Gaventa, *Acts* (Nashville: Abingdon, 2004), 355.

4. C. K. Barrett, *The Acts of the Apostles* (Edinburgh, Scotland: T & T Clark, 1998), 1208–1209.